# WHAT

# Treasured Memories of Alderville First Nation

### by Ruth Clarke
### & members of the community

*Ruth Clarke* (signature)

"Stories have to be told or they die, and when they die, we can't remember who we are or why we are here."

—August Boatwright in THE SECRET LIFE OF BEES by Sue Monk Kidd

**Sweetgrass Studios
Alderville First Nation**

# A Sweetgrass Studios Publication
114 Vimy Ridge Road
R.R.#2, Roseneath, Ontario, K0K 2X0 Canada

Copyright © 2006

All rights reserved.
No part of this book may be reproduced or transmitted in any form by any means without permission from the publisher.

Sweetgrass Studios trade paperback ISBN 0-9730420-4-4

The Sweetgrass Studios World Wide Web site address is
www.rickbeaver.com

Library and Archives Canada has catalogued this edition as follows:

**Library and Archives Canada Cataloguing in Publication**

**Clarke, Ruth, 1950–**
 What we hold dear: treasured memories of Alderville First Nation/Ruth Clarke and members of the Alderville community.

Continues Before The Silence.
**ISBN 0973042044**

1. Ojibway Indians—Ontario-Alderville Region—History.I. Title.

**E99.C6C523 2006**      971.3'57      C2006-903046-4

**CONTENTS**

| | |
|---|---|
| Acknowledgements | 4 |
| Introduction | 5 |
| The Jingle Dress–A Prologue | 7 |
| Gate-gan's Trunk | 14 |
| *Manomin*–Wild Rice | 18 |
| Allan Salt | 20 |
| Alder's'ville | 25 |
| History of the Rice Lake Indians | 37 |
| Life On the Lake | 39 |
| Fred Simpson–Olympic Marathon Runner | 49 |
| Albert Smoke–1922 Boston Marathon | 52 |
| War | 53 |
| Moses Marsden 1870-1968 | 59 |
| The Service | 62 |
| Norman Marsden 1881-1957 | 63 |
| Alvin Hagar | 64 |
| Reflections from Bob Marsden 1923-2001 | 65 |
| Bill Bigwin 1910-1991 | 68 |
| War Monument | 71 |
| Sports and the Dirty Thirties | 74 |
| Alderville's 100th Anniversary: 1937 | 76 |
| Centennial Celebrations | 77 |
| Hunting and Gathering | 79 |
| Wild Rice | 83 |
| Borden Crowe 1905-1985 | 90 |
| Trapping | 93 |
| The Forties | 95 |
| The Fifties | 96 |
| George Beaver 1868-1956 | 101 |
| The Man With the Marvelous Tan | 102 |
| The Sixties | 104 |
| Alton and Fran Bigwin | 106 |
| The Seventies | 108 |
| The Eighties | 110 |
| When the Real Wandering Ended: 1985 | 111 |
| Rick Beaver | 114 |
| Hal Gray | 116 |
| The Nineties | 117 |
| Randy Paul Smoke | 119 |
| The New Millennium | 121 |
| Pulling Together: 2004 | 122 |
| John Loukes 1911-2002 | 124 |
| Epilogue | 128 |

# Acknowledgements

First and foremost, I am eternally grateful to the late John Loukes for inviting me, in 1989, to write the history of Alderville First Nation. I am only sorry that he didn't live to see the second volume. Since then, through the years, a number of chiefs and councilors have supported this project. *Chi miigwech* to Nora Bothwell, Wesley Marsden and Jim Bob Marsden for supporting my efforts. Thanks to the Alderville Community Trust for providing funding to Sweetgrass Studios to enable me to finish writing the book and for ACT's support in publishing the manuscript.

Many, many individuals in Alderville contributed photographs, memorabilia and research to enable me to flesh-out this book. I know that if I started to list them, I would leave someone out, so *chi miigwech* to all the members of Alderville First Nation for your cooperation, generosity and patience for this project that began in 1990.

My gratitude and appreciation to Maureen Dietrich, for her steadfast determination that this, the second volume, even though it has photographs, should also be written as a story. Her careful, discerning eyes, her patience and her expertise as an editor were invaluable when I lost perspective and was too immersed in the material to see my errors or omissions.

Thanks to the Peterborough Centennial Museum and Archives that provided photographs of various riverboats that plied Rice Lake long ago, and for photographs from Roy Studio that the museum now owns.

Thanks also to the United Church Archives which provided photographs of Allan Salt, William Case and his wife, Eliza, of John Sunday or Shawundais, of their tombstone, of the old Mission House and school and of the church and school/office building.

*Chi miigwech* to Rick Beaver, who has come to understand how this process takes me away, who forgives my absence, and with enduring patience is there when I return. *Miigwech*.

# Introduction

**WHAT WE HOLD DEAR: Treasured Memories of Alderville First Nation** continues in the style of BEFORE THE SILENCE, written from the point of view of fictional characters. BEFORE THE SILENCE depicted life for the Mississauga Ojibway during the period 1825–1875, including their migration from Grape Island to their settlement in Alderville. In photographs and narrative, WHAT WE HOLD DEAR resumes the story in the late 1800s and continues to present-day life in Alderville.

Two women figure prominently in WHAT WE HOLD DEAR. Aged but spry Kathleen Franklin or Gate-gan, as she is called, and Katie Chase, her great granddaughter, narrate the story. I chose the surnames Franklin and Chase to be their family names because though these names once existed in Alderville, they are not common today. Therefore it would be impossible for readers to try to place these characters realistically in the present-day community. Though Gate-gan and Katie are fictional, all that the two women discuss throughout the book is factual.

Members of the Alderville community share the byline on this, the second volume of their history. Mary Jane Muskratte Simpson's manuscript, LIFE ON THE LAKE, finished in 1953, is a valuable addition to the book, as are the interviews and research that Melody Crowe and Arlene Beaver conducted in 1981. Also included are university papers written and interviews transcribed by Dave Mowat, as well as memorabilia pulled from various scrapbooks, notably those of Melody Crowe and Dixie Crowe, and the late Moses Marsden and John Loukes.

Many photographs have been included, but they are only a small fraction of what exists. When making decisions between classic, period photographs versus more recent sports photographs that were often newspaper clippings, I opted for the classic shots.

All of the photographs, recipes, research, interviews and lore became threads of history woven into the fabric of the story. This would have been impossible to do without Gategan and Katie who breathe life into the story, and use the vernacular, the language of their Village.

Anyone who spends a long period of time in a community begins to hear the particular choice of words which are peculiar to their society, yet are fitting and accurate. Words like "bleak" to describe an unfortunate situation is an accurate choice of word that is part of the Alderville vernacular, as are "deadening" and "cheap". Coined expressions and inventions of words, nicknames, all are very local, and because this book is meant to read like an oral history, it would have been remiss not to season the story with some popular expressions.

Similarly, when identifying themselves, people in Alderville First Nation often refer to themselves as First Nations, Native, and or Indian. I have interchanged them where it seemed appropriate, in keeping with the period of time when it was used.     RC

# The Jingle Dress
—A Prologue

Hi there. My name is Kathleen Elizabeth Chase, but you can call me Katie. I was named after my great-grandmother Kathleen who lives with us, so calling us by the same name would be confusing to us both. Twenty years ago, when I was just learning to talk, I couldn't pronounce the R letters in "great-grandmother." I could only say Gate-gan, and since then, that's what everyone in our family has been calling her. It sort of sounds like an Ojibway word, doesn't it?

Here in Alderville you can have a half dozen names or more. A baby first receives a name that relates to what occurred or what his or her parents saw or experienced on the day he or she was born—perhaps Morning Star or Evening Star or Jumping Fawn. I was born in Toronto and my Mom always teases me that my first name was Streetcar.

Traditionally, a child is given a name during a naming ceremony at some point later in her childhood. It's like a christening when she is given a name that she will be known by formally. But also in our Ojibway culture, we can be known by more than that one name throughout our lives, nicknames that family and friends give us— maybe from the way we look or act, what we do, or even from the phonetic sound of our given names. In addition to my given names, I have lots of others, but let's not go there. I've suffered enough torment with my last name, let alone the other monikers I've been given.

In September, I will take another name when Clifford and I are married. I won't be losing my own name, but rather, I will be uniting my family name with his: Kathleen Chase Martin. Nor will I forfeit my Native status. This has not always been the case for First Nation peoples— because of the Indian Act, a bill forged by the government in the mid-1800s to assimilate us into a Euro-Canadian culture, one that would ultimately do away with reserves and us as distinct nations. At that time, Native people were wards of the state, and when a Native woman married a non-Native, she would automatically lose her Indian status and so would her children. She had to give up any land she owned on the reserve where she had lived all her life, she would also give up her membership, and when she died, she would be buried in a white man's cemetery.

    Conversely, if a non-Native woman married a Native man, she was automatically given Native status, as were her children. During the two world wars, when a Native enlisted, he became enfranchised, meaning that he had entered the assimilation process. What a bony concept; it seems more like disenfranchised to me.

    In 1956 the government deemed it possible for Native people to be Canadian citizens but it wasn't until 1977 that the National Indian Brotherhood was consulted for the first time regarding the Indian Act. Until that time, Native women, who in hunting and gathering societies had been responsible for contributing 60-80% of their family's sustenance, were at the mercy of patriarchal Victorian law whose attitude was that women were the delicate sex, and therefore, subordinates. Poor. Both aspects of the law adhered to the Victorian notion that a wife was property. This way of thinking continually eroded any possibility of strength on the reserves. Any Indian who achieved a university degree, who became a doctor, lawyer or minister had been, until 1985, automatically enfranchised. This legislation was enforced until it was finally rewritten as Bill C-31 in 1985. Gee, I was only a year old then, barely taking my first steps. We were living in Toronto. Mom had moved there when she married my father whose family had long been enfranchised. She's told me about that time away from home, how she missed her family and had felt dispossessed—so much so that my father couldn't tolerate her debilitating depression and left. Mom raised me and my older siblings, my brother Shane and sister Bonnie, alone.

I am what you would call, in genealogical terms, the ninth generation after *Ishpiniibin*, or Sarah, as she was christened by William Case in 1825. I am the tenth, counting Sarah's uncle *Shawundais*, or John Sunday's generation. My great-great grandmother Mary married Wilfred Franklin just before World War I in 1917. She was to have been enfranchised when he enlisted in the army but he was killed immediately he'd entered battle so she was able to remain on the reserve with her daughter Kathleen. My Gate-gan has remained here all her life. Her daughter, my grandmother, was born and raised on the reserve, but then she married a non-Native and had to leave too. She also moved to Toronto where she tried to fit in, though she says she always felt like an alien there. Her marriage broke up but she couldn't go home until we all moved back here in 1986. Thinking about it now it feels like I am remembering some ancient history, but it was only 20 years ago that things had changed.

With the passage of Bill C-31 in 1985, overnight, my mother, along with thousands of other Native women across Canada who had married non-Native men and had to give up property and status on their reserves, all of them were able to regain their status and return to the membership of their band. That day, even my own status as a baby changed. In a very short time, we moved back to Alderville. First, we rented a cottage at Vimy Ridge, and then we had this house built.

I have always been lucky. Having been born in the 1980s, the only real poverty I ever saw was on television, and it was somewhere far away. Exotic poverty. I was fortunate to go to school when Native heritage was being given attention – and was celebrated. That certainly hasn't always been the way. Alderville exists as a community because originally it had been settled to be the Mecca of Indian Missions–and became the prototype for residential schools... using measures that silenced Native people from speaking their language and practising their culture. That happened a long time ago, and much has changed since then. Now it's okay for me to study and speak Ojibway, to practise traditional ways, to openly celebrate my culture. In being able to do this, I have realized *Ishpiniibin's* prophetic dream of future generations of her people dancing in full regalia around their village drum.

A few years ago, I made my own jingle dress for the first annual pow wow here in 1995. Our dear departed Lily Bourgeois used to travel down from the Curve Lake reserve to give us teachings about the significance of what we were creating and the symbolism that our outfits held. I learned that the jingle dress originated in mid-western Canada, in an area called Lake of the Woods, where a young woman had been ill. One of her relatives, her father or grandfather, had a vision of a dress covered in shells. In his vision, he was told that the dress held healing powers and should be worn for that purpose in ceremonial healing dances. The jingles were later made from snuff cans bent into cones and sewn onto the dress. Boy, they must have *snuffed* a lot in those days. Today we use replicas of those snuff boxes, though some women still use shells. Jingle dancers are given *semaa*–the Ojibway word for tobacco–when they are asked to dance for someone who is ill, or in need of spiritual healing, or sometimes they are asked to honour a loved one who has passed away. When we dance a jingle dance, other dancers stand out of respect and honour for the healing dress and our dance.

In between sessions with Lily, we all worked on our outfits at home. That winter while I was sewing my dress, Gate-gan used to sit in her rocking chair next to the stove, rocking and watching me. Each evening before I started sewing, I burned sweetgrass and smudged us both, to prepare us for the evening. While I was sewing, I often told her what I had just learned at school while I'd been doing research for a paper, some tradition or practice that I'd never heard of, and Gate-gan would illustrate– bring it to life– with her recollections.

I had been working on a paper about the important role Native women played in the traditional hunting and gathering society and came across a passage about Alderville women going off with their children in early spring to collect maple sap and process it into syrup and sugar blocks that they stored in boxes they made from birch bark. It turns out that Gate-gan was one of those women. She told me about a sugar bush they went to on the north shore of Rice Lake. The first generation of our ancestors who settled here in 1837 would have been the only ones to know what Rice Lake looked like before the lock at Hastings was constructed in the mid-1800s. That same year they settled here was when the Trent Canal system was proposed from Quinte to Rice Lake. I've read somewhere that the level of the lake rose six to eight feet up the shoreline, so I'd expect that Gate-gan and the other women were actually further inland than their ancestors, past what the old timers called the "Drowned Lands".

Normally, the women went there some time in March when the sun's strength started to pull the sap into the branches of the awakening maple trees. Can you picture the group travelling across the lake, some of them gliding across the ice with steel runners on their canoes, poling with specially fashioned paddles that were pointed and had steel tips for gouging into the ice? According to Gate-gan, Everett Simpson was known to be one of the best at making these paddles.

The men were out trapping at the same time, when muskrat, beaver and mink were active in the swamps, creeks and rivers that fed into Rice Lake. The men took many of the ice canoes to get to their traps before the ice went out of the lake, craft that would revert to regular water canoes if the ice did give way. Perhaps some of the men would deliver their women and children to the sugar bush en route to their trapping locales. Many women hiked across on snowshoes, often with babies on their backs and pulling toboggans with cauldrons and rigging for their time in the sugar bush. Kids who could walk played their way across the lake, propelled by some drama they had created. Some of the women travelled ahead of the others to tap the trees, pounding in basswood spigots they'd carved from branches. Beneath these taps they set pails to collect the dripping sap. Other women had been there in advance, to cut wood for the endless fires needed to boil down the sap, to evaporate the water and reduce it to a golden syrup. What is the figure: 40 liters of sap are required to boil down to one liter of syrup?

Gate-gan also told me about a non-Native woman who lived near the sugar bush. She visited them at their camp each year "to see the new crop of Indian babies" hanging on the branches of trees in their bundle-boards—our women's way of setting up daycare in the woods, where sphagnum moss was in endless supply for use as disposable diapers.

After that, Gate-gan says the sugar bush near the Indian Fields and Norman's Pond on the reserve were tapped, and all the kids went there after school each day to help collect sap or wood. Their reward was maple taffy that would form in sweet amber strings when their mothers drizzled some of the boiling syrup on the snow for them.

One day this spring some of us went for a walk through those woods and I found an old glass ink bottle that students used when they had nib pens, before fountain pens. It was filled with mud and when I cleaned it out I found that it was perfectly intact. There was a little well on one side of the bottle where you could wipe off any excess globules of ink from the nib before you started to write. I imagined children hiking back after school to join their mothers in the sugar bush. Maybe they would put their school books in a hollow knot or the crotch of a tree–there would still be some snow in the woods, and they would want to keep their books dry. Maybe the ink pot had fallen into the snow around the base of the tree, and the kid would not be able to do his homework. He would worry all night about the punishment, probably a caning, that would greet him at school the next morning.

When I got weary of sewing and packed my dress away for the night, Gate-gan always hugged me hard and kissed me good night, then she shuffled off to her room where I often heard her dragging out her old trunk and fussing in the depths of it. I always wanted to see what she kept in there but felt too cheap to ask, and now I'm glad I didn't.

I finally finished my jingle dress and have worn it at every pow-wow since our first one in 1995. The first had to be held at the community centre because of a rainstorm that prevented us from dancing outside. Then a few pow-wows were held Canada Day weekend at the baseball park. The heat was oppressive those years, the air so muggy and heavy with moisture that we were often dripping with perspiration. But now the pow-wow committee has its own land and yesterday we could have used some of the heat of previous years.

This year, it was downright chilly and damp during the pow-wow. It had rained for days before, and the grounds were soggy. Deadening for the campers. Our family had all gone there together, four generations of us, but early in the afternoon Gate-gan asked Mom to give her a ride home. She said she was chilled to the bone and wanted to take a nap with her hot water bottle, but she had other plans, the little scamp.

        The rest of us stayed at the pow-wow all day and feasted there that night. I danced every dance under *Nokomis*, Grandmother Moon, as she bathed us in her fullness. She lit our way home much, much later in the evening. Every one of the dancers seemed to have been energized with each dance, connected with Mother Earth on which they danced to the pounding drums that symbolize her heartbeat.

        It was only when the drums ceased, when the air was still, that we started to feel fatigued. When I arrived home, Gate-gan's light was still on but her door was closed. That meant she wasn't to be disturbed, for she always sleeps with her door open. So I crashed without saying goodnight. I remember feeling such a sweet exhaustion that I'm sure I conked out as soon as my head hit the pillow.

From "A Good Place to Gather" painting by Randy Paul Smoke 2001

# Gate-gan's Trunk

When we got up the morning after the pow-wow, the sun was strong and the air was clear, hot and dry. Too bad we hadn't had this weather yesterday for the pow-wow. After we'd all eaten breakfast, Mom, Shane, Bonnie and Grandma packed into the car and moved to the lake. They'll be there for the rest of the month, their turn at the cottage that was left to Mom and her four siblings to share.

It's a cool arrangement because Uncle Reg prefers to be there in the winter. He loves to ice fish. Aunt Mary likes to come in the spring and early summer when birds return and raise their families. When flocks of ducks arrive from the mid-eastern coast of the United States to fatten-up on the riches of Rice Lake before continuing their journey to their breeding grounds on the prairies and beyond. Uncle Vinnie likes coming to the cottage in the fall because he's a hunter and he gets the ducks on their return trip. So there's never any problem with scheduling stays at the cottage. We've gone there together every summer but this year Gate-gan and I decided to stay here and, as she says, "batch it." It isn't like the cottage is that far away. I can bicycle there in 15 minutes if I start to suffer from familial withdrawal. Not.

Gate-gan and I are suddenly alone in the quiet house. We clear the breakfast things from the table and Gate-gan starts running water in the sink. We stand together, comfortable in our silence, her washing, me drying.

"This is the last big stack of dishes that we'll have to do for the next few weeks," Gate-gan says as she finishes drying her hands and hanging the towel on the oven door to dry. She starts trundling off, then stops and turns to me.

"I've got something I want to show you." She tugs me toward her room. For such a tiny woman, she is very strong. She has pushed her trunk to the edge of her bed and motions me to sit down on one side of it. She sits on the other, reaches for my hand and looks at me with her sparkling jet black eyes.

"It is said, my dear, that timing is everything and before you embark on the next path on your life's journey this fall, your marriage to Cliff, it is time for me to give you your legacy."

Some brides-to-be are given cedar hope chests that they are meant to fill with their handiwork and gifts they receive—embroidery and the like, that they can use to adorn their new homes. I know Gate-gan well enough to know that what we were about to look at wouldn't be doilies.

"You know that this trunk was made by one of our ancestors on Grape Island," she begins.

"And that your great-grandmother, Sarah, *Ishpiniibin*, gave it to you," I add.

"That is correct. And now it is time for *your* great grandmother to give this trunk to you."

I gasp, speechless. When we first moved here, we used this flat-topped trunk as a coffee table and I heard about its history, or provenance, as they say on the Antiques Roadshow. When we got a new coffee table, Gate-gan took the trunk to her bedroom. Many times I tried to conjure the trunk's storied journey from Grape Island, southeast of here on Lake Ontario, all the way to its new home. Sometimes, in my mind's eye, I would see it being loaded with Aunt Sarah's belongings. It would have been heavy with pieces of china that the Methodists in Britain had given the mission after one of its fundraising efforts abroad. Maybe all the pieces would be wrapped in one of the quilts that Sarah had stitched together from scraps of woven wool left from the men's suits she and the other girls had made—from scratch, including raising the sheep. The quilt would keep them warm in their new bed. I imagined that the trunk would still exude a fragrant blend of pine and sheep lanolin.

Two people probably lugged the trunk down to the water's edge. Hopefully, they'd had a dock. It would have been carefully set in the middle of the canoe for the paddle from Lake Ontario, up the Trent River to Rice Lake. I imagined that sometimes the waves licked the gunnels of the canoe and splashed against the sides of the trunk. There would have been a portage before it reached Alderville. Or maybe it had had the luxury of riding on a wagon behind a team of horses once it got to the shore of Lake Ontario, though it isn't likely. Chipped in places, scuffed and worn, the trunk has endured 175 years and is still very sound.

"In this trunk I have been keeping precious things: what we hold dear, Katie, pieces of our documented history, about our people and their lives. I've kept clippings, photographs, medals, recipes, remedies and memorabilia from further back than I can remember. Students here in the Village have given me transcripts of interviews they have conducted with elders and other members of the community, and papers they have written in university Native Studies courses since they were first initiated. I've kept them all.

"Over the years, as you've been growing up, you have shown me that your Native heritage is precious to you and that you live it daily. I saw you dance yesterday in the jingle dress you made. I even watched you make that dress and alter it as you have filled out over the past few years. I have been most impressed with the way you conduct your life, Katie, and I have decided that it is time for me to give you this trunk and everything in it, for now I am very sure that you will take care of it like I have."

Together we lift the lid of the trunk. Mementos of ten generations lie in seemingly arbitrary, though sometimes chronological, layers. The pieces span eras, marking times, much like an ancient tree trunk when it is cut, revealing its age in rings, or like layers in an archeological dig.

A braid of sweetgrass lies curled on top of a number of typed pages.

"The hair of Mother Earth," Gate-gan whispers, " her gift to the *Anishinabeg* people, still as fragrant as the day I received it last summer. As you know, sweetgrass symbolizes kindness. It was given to me when I was an honoured guest at an elders' conference. When I received the sweetgrass that day and breathed in its fragrance, I started thinking about the greater symbols that the braid signifies. And I felt like I was filled to the brim, so bursting with courage and pride, that I was able to share my thoughts and tell them to the whole group gathered in the auditorium. Do you know our teaching about the braid?

"Alone, one little strand of sweetgrass is weak and might break under stress, but braided it becomes strong and can't be broken. Perhaps our ancestors wore their hair in braids to symbolize their strength," Gate-gan suggests.

"Someone once told me that Native men wear a single braid to signify that they are bachelors, two braids to let women know they're married, sort of organic wedding rings," I muse, looking at the diamond sparkling on my left hand. "Today couples don't marry or divorce as easily as they did then either," I recall from my research.

"In some cultures, couples merely repeat the phrase, 'I marry you,' three times to each other, to make the marriage vow. And in the old days, for an Indian to divorce, the act of putting their spouse's *mocassins* outside the *wiigwaam* meant the end of the marriage. Pretty simple, eh? No officials or lawyers."

"Today," Gate-gan points out, "many couples don't even bother with those simple symbols, let alone traditional weddings in a church. Any way, you and Cliff are, and for that I am happy. Now it is time to light this braid of sweetgrass so that we may clear the path for your new journey." Gate-gan strikes a wooden match against the rusty hinge of the trunk and holds the flame under the braid until it smolders and catches fire. When it is burning sufficiently, she blows it out and guides the issuing smoke from the braid over her own head and shoulders, and then mine.

"*Chi miigwech*, Gate-gan."

Gate-gan smudges us and the room, cleansing our minds and clearing them of impure or negative thoughts, preparing us for what we are about to do. The fragrance of the burning grass comforts and calms me as I draw wisps of the smoke over me like I am bathing. When she has finished, Gate-gan extinguishes the braid by snuffing it in an abalone shell on her bookshelf. She stands erect as a soldier, facing me.

"As the unofficial retiring curator of this small but important museum, I officially appoint you, Kathleen Elizabeth Chase, my successor, a lifetime position that I hope you will accept and ultimately pass on to future generations. Cherish what we hold dear, Katie."

"I accept, and I will do my best to care for them as you have, Gate-gan." She sits down on the bed again and after fluffing her pillows against the head-board, she leans back, folds her hands in her lap and watches me.

## *Manomin*—Wild Rice

It is as if Gate-gan has ordered the contents of the trunk for me. The first piece is a recent transcript of a discussion that cousins Rick and Jeff Beaver had with Dave Mowat a few years ago, when he was trying to piece together an oral history of the relationship between the Ojibways of Grape Island and the Algonquins of Ardoch. As I read the transcript it becomes clear that what they said sets out the historical background and significance of Rice Lake to the First Nations. During their discussions, an Ontario road map must have been laid on the table, because first off, everyone agrees to try to ignore the roads and highways that wouldn't have existed, and to focus on the rivers and tributaries that laced the country together for Native people. A map accompanies the transcript, and I open it up on the bed between Gate-gan and myself so that I can refer to places they mention.

I read that Rice Lake's wild rice history dates back more than 9,000 years according to soil samples taken from the lake bed in the 1970s by Walter Kenyon, an archeologist from the Royal Ontario Museum in Toronto. Historically, the lake had been faster moving because of the glacial flow. And it seems that in each period of aboriginal history, everyone has been here. It was a rich place where they were able to dig clams, hunt ducks and geese and gather wild rice. The Mohawks once lived where the Hiawatha reserve is now located on the north shore of Rice Lake, and the Mohawks harvested wild rice and grew corn. A big settlement of theirs has been found at Serpent Mounds. I knew that.

The transcript discusses that in the late 1600s, the Mississauga Ojibway came down from their traditional territory on the north shore of Georgian Bay and fought the Mohawks. Ontario had been a meeting place for all Algonquin speaking peoples, Ojibway being one. There was a lot of communication among the Algonquin, Ojibway, Odawa and Pottawattami, who were all allies in that war. They would have had to rely on people, particularly the Odawas, traders, who were still trading with the East Coast after eight or nine hundred years. The Pottawattami were fire-keepers at the Three Fires Confederacy Councils, fire symbolizing unification among all disparate groups.

The Odawas had knowledge of routes–what we call the Ottawa River (Matawa to Montreal) being the major one. Our people would have known a lot of territory because of their travels, trade and connections. For them, their canoes were their messengers, race cars, barges, and war canoes. Different canoe designs were made for different reasons, to enable them to move freely, but traditionally, birch bark and cedar canoes weighing only 30 pounds were used because they were the easiest to manage and repair.

Both Jeff and Rick's ancestors can trace their recorded history to the Grape Island Methodist settlement, when our people were called the Kingston and Ganonoque Mississauga Ojibway (Kingston and Ganonoque being the areas they inhabited, Mississauga meaning mouths of rivers and Ojibway referring to the puckered stitching in the mocassins they wore) and to the Algonquins at Ardoch. The Ardoch-Grape Island connection had probably already been established because of water travel at that time and Ardoch is on a main water course. When our ancestors made their final migration to Alderville, they would have come the same way–paddling and camping at the same spots. They'd set traps at night to have small game for the next morning's meal. There were tons of fish. Since our traditional lands had been around Lake Ontario for more than 300 years, they would have known those routes. The cousins pointed out that the Trent system has a lot of tributaries in Algonquin Park–a radial flow. Once you get on the shoulders of the park, you can travel anywhere. And they did. They followed water and trails, they knew political boundaries defined by the Grand Councils, others by marriages.

Dave Mowat said that according to people from there, Ardoch had always been a meeting area for the Ojibway and Algonquins, not necessarily a settlement. It was close to the Ottawa River, Mazinaw Lake and the Madawaska, where Rick, Jeff and Dave's ancestors were employed as loggers and guides at fishing and hunting lodges. Ardoch's rice had originally been taken there by the Ojibway from Alderville; it has been proven by looking at the rice's genetics, which are the same as what grew in Rice Lake. People took wild rice and roots or seeds from medicinal plants with them to plant along their route so the plants they needed would be there upon their return–their supermarket and pharmacy. Here, the transcript ends.

"Don't you have the rest of this, Gate-gan?" I ask.

"You'll come to it later. Just keep going, Katie."

# Allan Salt
# 1818-1911

**Rev. Allan Salt**
Courtesy United Church Archives/
Victoria University Archives,
Toronto 76.001P/5760 N

Gate-gan leans toward me as I pick up Allan Salt's photograph. "He's always been my hero. What an accomplished, honourable and dedicated man he was. The poor lad's mother died, perhaps on Grape Island, when he was very small. Allan's father remarried but his new wife was unkind to Allan, and somehow he got himself adopted by William Case and lived on Grape Island.

"He must have been a brilliant little boy, for at the age of eight he was speaking before large groups of non-Native people at fundraising events in Belleville, reading from the Bible and singing with the other children. He migrated with everyone else from Grape Island to Alderville in the late 1830s. Whether it was Case's plan for him to be a teacher, or Allan's own decision, I don't know, but he went off to Toronto to teachers' college and graduated from Toronto Normal School in 1848, when he was 30 years old. He returned to Alderville to work at the Industrial School that was here in those days. The residential school was operating then too, though attendance was dwindling. People were dying from cholera, and if surviving children ever did get a chance to go home and visit their parents, they never returned."

Gate-gan leaned back on her pillows and crossed her arms. "During the cholera epidemic," she continued, "Allan helped in the hospital here, attending to patients, and in the process contracted something, whether it was cholera, or not, I don't know, but he went comatose. The Indians thought he was dead, but his wife wouldn't believe it and persuaded them to leave Allan another day. They agreed.

A second day passed, and on the third day when they were approaching the bed to remove his body for burial, Allan must have gathered all the energy he had, for he sat up in bed, just for a second, then fell back. He told people later that he had heard them talking, and though he hadn't been able to respond, he had prayed silently that if God would spare him from being buried alive, he would devote his life to promoting religion among his people.

"Well, Katie, Allan Salt honoured his promise to God, serving as a missionary among Native people at many of the missions in more remote areas. He was ordained as deacon in 1854 and for the next 30 years, he served at three missions and the Muncey residential school, until he finally settled at Parry Island, where he served until he was retired in 1901.

"Allan Salt also collected medicines when he lived here in Alderville and later on Walpole Island. His granddaughters have a copy of a manuscript he wrote during those years and gave me a copy. Many of the plants have Ojibway names but few people know what they are. Maybe you will be able to find out.

"All his papers are here, Katie. He was very prolific. I have copies of everything from the National Archives in Ottawa, photocopies of his journals and writings of traditional ways, papers that our family and other people have brought me over the years. I even have one of his remedies."

---

*A Wash for Inflammation*

1/2 ounce sugar lead (sumac?)
1/2 pint whisky
1/2 pint vinegar

Put in a quart bottle and fill bottle with water. For inflammation and bruises.

"Allan Salt's son, Thomas, married Maria Marsden," Gate-gan explains as we look at a photo taken in Saugeen, Ontario, in the summer of 1903. The gentleman standing in the centre is James Marsden. To his left, his wife, Sofia. Seated is her mother, Mrs. Madwayosh. To her left, Sofia's sister, Eleanor. Sofia's daughter Maria Salt (married to Allan's son, Thomas Salt) is seated at the far right. On the lawn are Thomas and Maria Salt's children, Edith and her brother Thomas. Rufus Marsden is to the right of the window.

"What I find so interesting about Allan Salt is that although he was a devout Methodist for all those years, it appears that he never denied his cultural heritage," Gate-gan continues, pointing to his Ojibway name beneath his English name on the tombstone where he is buried on Parry Island. "The National Archives have all of his notebooks in which he writes about Mississauga religion. His manuscript on medicinal plants is written in English, but the names of the plants are Ojibway. He seemed to be able to live his life completely, embracing both cultures."

Next on the pile lies an old photograph of Allan Salt's benefactor, William Case, and Case's second wife, Eliza. According to a note written on the back of it, at Rev. Case's request, he was buried in the Alderville Cemetery. A monument was erected in his memory, with the inscription, "Sacred to the memory of Rev. William Case, the Father of Canadian Methodist Missions to the Indian Tribes. Died at Alderville, October 19,1855 in the 76th year of his life and the 50th year of his ministry."

**Rev. William Case with Mrs. Case**
Courtesy United Church Archives/Victoria University Archives 76.001P/937N

**Monument to Case and Sunday of the Methodist Indian Mission**
Courtesy United Church Archives/Victoria University Archives, Toronto  90.162P/54 N  [n. d.]

**John Sunday**
Courtesy United Church Archives/Victoria University Archives, Toronto
76.001P/6453 N [n. d.]

I recognize the sketch of *Shawundais*, or John Sunday, as he was christened by the Methodists. He was one of the first of our people to be converted to Christianity. He was a renowned orator who went on to be an itinerant missionary. On the back of John Sunday's photograph, I read that he was buried beside Rev. Case and the reverse side of the monument was inscribed to him: "Sacred to the memory of Rev. John Sunday, a Chief of the Ojibway Indians, one of the earliest of Father Case's converts and a most useful and intelligent and faithful missionary. Died at Alderville, December 14, 1875." No one could ever pin down when John was born. He said he fought in the war of 1812. Let's say if he was only 15 when he went off to fight, he would have been 78 in 1875.

A third side of the monument carries the inscription: "These Holy and Apostolic men laid large foundations, and others having been largely thereupon. This memorial is erected by Ministers of the Methodist Conference and the Alderville Indians." Apparently, a Reverend Sparling, one of the ministers who preached at the church, died here later and is buried beside the other two ministers.

# ALDER 'S' VILLE

Catherine Franklin

The next piece is a yellowed clipping from a Montreal newspaper published in 1890, noting that Catherine C. Franklin, an "Indian" girl, had won the Northumberland County essay contest. She had written about Alderville's beginnings when they were settled by the Methodists on Grape Island. I'd seen a photocopy of this essay, but not the original newspaper clipping from that period. I smell the paper for traces of ink, a smell that I love, but that was long gone.

In her essay, Catherine Franklin describes life on Grape Island, its popularity and overpopulation and her people's subsequent selection of 1214.10 hectares, or 3,000 acres, in Alnwick Township, Northumberland County, to build a new settlement. Catherine writes that *"five young men were sent [from Grape Island] to view the land. When they returned, they reported that the land was good. As a result, in the year 1833, a company of 40 started with their axes and arriving on the reserve, commenced chopping a space of 20 rods [100 meters or 330 feet] wide for [about three kilometers or] one and a half miles. A saw mill was built in the same year to mill lumber for the construction of the 40 houses they planned to build. The first sawyer that ran the mill was the father of John Thackeray who is now Indian Agent of this band. In the same year, the Rev. Robert Alder from England visited the village and called it after his own name. Ever since it has gone by the name of Aldersville."* ( Somewhere along the line, the S in Alderville got dropped. I read on....)

*"In 1834 a final settlement was made. When the Indians settled on the reserve they numbered over 500. Of those, only 11 are now living who moved from Grape Island, viz., Rev. Allan*

Salt, Rev. Henry Chase, George Blaker, George Comego, Francis Beaver, Mitchell Chubb, Thomas Marsden, Peggy James, Sarah Ann Franklin, Mary Simpson and Eliza Shipegaw. The present number of Indians now living on the reserve , however, numbers only about 200."

"Reverend Henry Chase was one of my father's ancestors," I realize and look at Gate-gan. "And your husband's ancestor, Sarah Ann, was from Grape Island too."

"Yes, we all had beginnings there," Gate-gan replies. "And given the diseases and hardships they had from the time they moved here, until 1890, it isn't surprising that so few of the Grape Island people were alive 56 years later."

From the look of this early map of Alnwick Township, we've been able to trade or buy waterfront property since then. A current map of Alderville within Alnwick Township would look sort of like a patchwork quilt.

In the old days, our ancestors were meant to quit hunting, fishing and trapping. Poor. Oh, that's backward. Our people have always been hunters and gatherers. Even the settlers who owned property on the shores of Rice Lake knew this and often suggested that they trade their waterfront for other land that the band owned so our people could get to the lake and have a place to launch their canoes. To move here from an island on Lake Ontario, to be made to give up, to ignore the bounties of the land and the seasons, wouldn't that be hard on the nerves? To have to turn around and become farmers, trying to grow crops on land that previous settlers had abandoned because the sandy soil couldn't be cultivated– now what was that all about?

On May 6, 1875, through a band council resolution, all farms on the reserve were to be leased out to "white men" unless there were Indians willing to work their own farms. In the agreement, they were required to commit to farming for not less than five years and for no more than 10 years before the agreement would be reviewed again.

The women had resumed working on their crafts, and even much later, many women like Katharine Gray made beautiful baskets, and many younger women continue to bead and make crafts today. In her manuscript, Mary Jane Muskratte Simpson (known in the community as Aunt Min) a descendant of John Simpson from Grape Island, describes some of the work they did.

*"In earlier days much of the work fell to the women, who, in addition to their regular duties, braided corn husks into door mats, peeled strips of ash to the desired thickness and wove them into baskets. They made boxes and small canoes of birch bark, with intricate designs embroidered with porcupine quills. These were bound with a sweet-scented grass..."*

Katharine Gray's baskets

**1888 Alderville Chief & Council**
(back row standing)
Councilors: Thomas Marsden, Peter Crowe, Francis Beaver
(front row seated) Councilor George Blaker, Indian Agent John Thackeray, Chief Mitchell Chubb, Secretary William Loukes.

Catherine Franklin mentions that at the time she was writing her essay in 1890, the chief of Alderville was Mitchell Chubb, one of the original people from Grape Island.

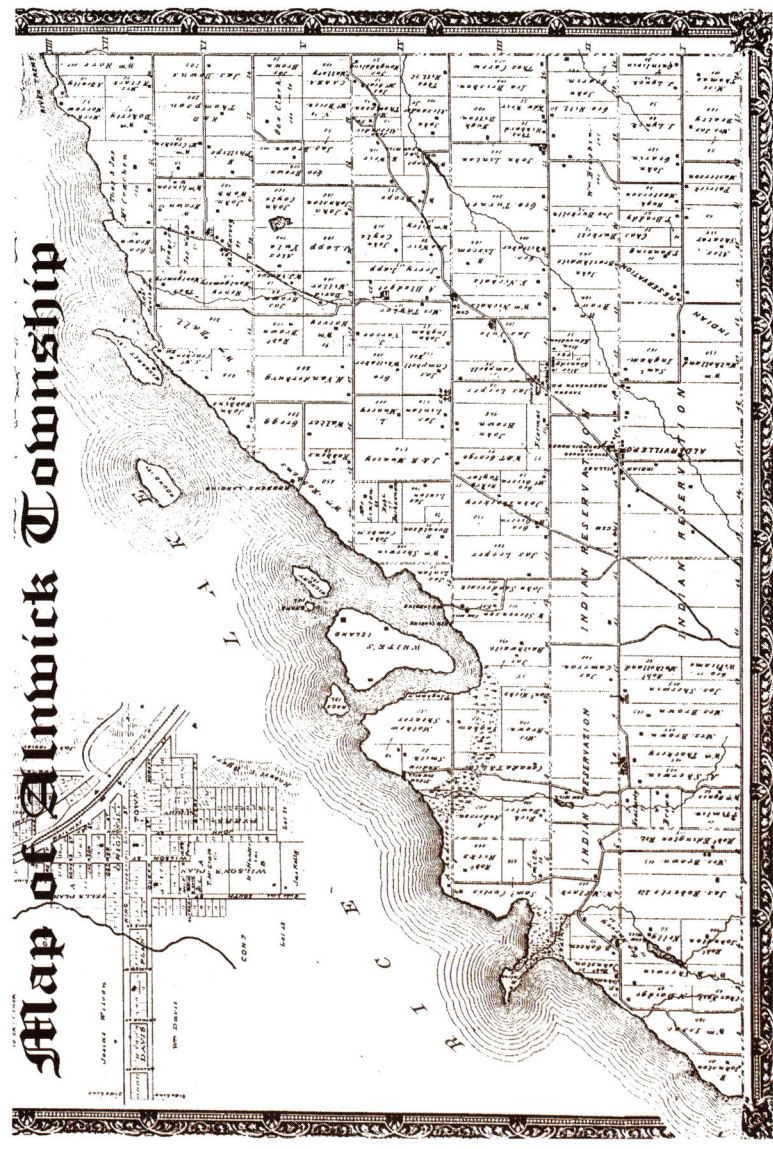

Gate-gan leans over the map. "It wasn't until 1914 that Alderville was able to purchase waterfront. Look at the shoreline and you'll see that a large swath, 38 acres of lakeshore opposite White's Island on Rice Lake, was once owned by a man named Linton. Somewhere there's a copy of the resolution that the band purchased the property for the sum of $800.00. Apparently, some time later, there was a naming contest and the area was named Vimy Ridge, honouring Alderville's veterans who had fought in World War I. Many people have permanent homes and cottages there now, including ours, but these old photographs give you an idea of what the lake looked like years ago. Jack Louke's white frame two-storey cottage is one of the ones built at that time."

**Hunters on Rice Lake** circa 1907" Bill Muskrat (left), George Potash, Alfred Crowe, Pook Anderson

More photos showed what the Village looked like in the old days. According to Catherine Franklin, the church organist was paid $40 and the sexton or caretaker, $60 annually. Jumpin'. That wouldn't buy much. The resident missionary was paid for by the Methodist Missionary Society, so that would help the band out. The brick buildings have long since disappeared. The one by the church once doubled as a council hall upstairs and school house on the ground floor.

Exterior of Mission School (right) and Church.
Circa 1920s
Courtesy United Church Archives/Victoria University Archives, Toronto
90.162P/55 N

Former mission house & school

Courtesy United Church Archives/ Victoria University Archives,
Toronto. 1948 September 7
90.162P/51 S

Though the Mission House was built some time later than the church and hall, it was turned into a hospital for a time, according to Alvin Hagar and Bob Marsden who told Gate-gan wild stories about whole groups of kids, en masse, all having their tonsils taken out, like cutting the tails off all the lambs in the spring. They said that Dr. Armstrong took the tonsils out with a contraption like a sewing machine that Alf Simpson peddled while Dr. Armstrong did the dirty work. Alvin remembers counting to 14 before he went out from the anesthetic. And once the operation was completed, Alvin said, the kids went home, I expect with no bowls of ice cream.

**"Mississauga School Alderville" 1911**

Robert Tobico (left), unknown man, Lillian Crowe, Eliza Smoke, Louise Chubb, unknown, Mr. Joblin, Maude Crowe, Alberta Crowe, unknown man, Viola Gray, Ben Chubb, Jack Tobico. Middle: Gertrude Marsden (left), unknown, Helen Crowe, 2 unknown boys, Cecil Gray holding sign, 2 unknown boys, Chester Beaver, (unknown girl behind), Mary Crowe, Stella Crowe. Front row: Howard Smoke (left), Walter Crowe, Cecil Marsden, 3 unknown, Irene Smoke, Earl Smoke, Wally Marsden, Hartley Franklin, Peter Crowe, Borden Crowe

June 4, 1912 School Photo

Gate-gan chuckles as I put a series of photographs together and lay them across my knees.

"That big man is William Loukes," she explains. "In fact, he appears earlier with the chief and council of 1888." She points to him and his family. " He was the father of John, Allie and Ellen, and he owned that house on the left. He was one of the men from the Village who continued to farm and made a go of it. The house on the right in both pictures was originally owned by my great Uncle Bob Franklin, and then Bob Marsden Senior owned it. He ran a general store that was a popular meeting place.

"In later years," Gate-gan says, "Allie Loukes ran the post office which was also such an attractive hangout that Allie is said to have sprinkled sulphur on the top of the stove to smoke the loiterers out of the place. You'd think the smell of his cigars would have been enough. In addition to being postmaster, he cut hair and ran a craft shop where he sold braids of sweetgrass, among other things. Just thinking about him, my memories of Allie combine the smells of sweetgrass and cigars," Gate-gan reminisces. "What a character. Darn good baseball player too."

William Loukes circa 1914

William Loukes & family. Allie at bottom on the right, next to his brother John circa 1916

The Village (above) and Allie Loukes' Store circa 1920s

"Annuity Day was a really big event here on the reserve," Gate-gan says when she finds a shot of "Uncle Bob" Marsden. "And shopkeepers were into I guess what you'd call deficit financing. People like Uncle Bob would sell us groceries and dry goods throughout the year, putting us "on tick" which meant that we didn't pay for it at the time, but he'd keep the amounts we owed by our names, and when the Indian Agent came around on Annuity Day to give us our cheques, Uncle Bob and other store owners like him would tally up our debts and they would get their money."

"Uncle Bob" Marsden circa 1950

The ghostly figure standing behind the top row of girls is Mr. Wilding who taught at the school from 1924–1929, so this photograph was taken some time during those five years. The first girl is Sarah Marsden (left), then Marg Franklin, Nina Lake, Reta Marsden, Elmira Beaver, Ellen Loukes. Second row: Isabelle Sunday, Olive Lake, Queenie Smoke, Bessie Chase, Evelyn Simpson, Elsie Smoke, Mildred Franklin, Alice Beaver, Irene Beaver. Third row: Gerald Franklin (left), Osborne Beaver, Alvin Hagar, Roy Smoke, Robert Smoke, Amos Blaker, Jack Loukes, Cliff Smoke. Fourth row: Bill Wilding (left), Bill Marsden, Dan Simpson, Art Beaver, Harold Wilding, Alvin Beaver

Mae (left) and Lucy Simpson 1920s

Jack Simpson in 1930s

"Lucy, Mae and Jack Simpson were siblings, three of the eight children Susan and Fred Simpson had," Gate-gan explains.

"Lucy Lovena Simpson Crowe suffered from goiters," Gate-gan says, leaning back, and gazing off into some unknown memory. "We've had a lot of superstitions over the years, you know, Katie."

"I know a few of them, like when a bird flies into your house it's a sign that someone is going to die."

"Yes, well, that's one. Lucy believed that letting a grass snake slither over her neck would cure her goiters. And you know, something? It did."

"Sort of like rubbing a toad over your warts is supposed to make them go away," I remember from my childhood affliction, when Granny used to suggest that remedy, probably knowing full well that I was afraid of toads, as well as frogs and snakes.

"Something like that," Gate-gan says. "Her grandson Dave told me about her leaning back in her rocking chair while one of her children placed a snake on her neck."

"And goiters were all from the lack of iodized salt in the diet," I say, shivering at the thought of the snake, and grateful we've made advances in science. Gate-gan knows all about my childhood fears and thankfully she says nothing.

# History of the Rice Lake Indians
by Mary Jane Muskratte Simpson

"That manila envelope is the largest package you'll find in the trunk," Gate-gan tells me as I open it. It contains a copy of Mary Jane Muskratte Simpson's manuscript– also known as Aunt Min, her HISTORY OF THE RICE LAKE INDIANS. "She wrote it in 1953 and dedicated it to her son, Everett Simpson whom you'll meet later," Gate-gan explains.

The old envelope is ripped and the manuscript dog-eared and stained, she's read it so many times. With the manuscript, an article published in a 1964 edition of The [United Church] Observer describes this prolific writer who, in addition to writing articles and manuscripts, also corresponded with pen-pals around the globe. The article tells how Mary had dealt with one pen-pal who would lapse into his Czechoslovakian language when writing her. Mary retaliated by writing back in Ojibway; her point was taken by her pen-pal, and she never had to have the Czech's letters translated again.

The interviewer describes Mary Jane Muskratte Simpson's voyage in a canoe from Hiawatha, when as a new bride, she paddled with Alf, her husband, to their new home in Alderville. She became a member of the county historical society, she addressed many women's groups, travelled to other reserves to help organize new Homemaker Clubs for Indian women, the Native equivalent of chapters of Women's Institutes, that offer fellowship and assistance in the aspects of homemaking and domestic life. In addition, she wrote weekly columns for the Cobourg Sentinel Star.

Mary Jane Muskratte Simpson is photographed for an interview by Joyce Knudsen in The Observer, September 15, 1964

"The men from Grape Island and Alderville have always been known for their oratory and storytelling, but it appears that the women were communicators too," I remark to Gate-gan.

"Ah yes, Katie, "Gate-gan muses philosophically. "We write because we are really generally quite shy and quiet. Eeee," she throws her head back, laughing until her shoulders shake and tears come to her eyes. Then she straightens up and looks at the manuscript in my hands.

"'Life On The Lake' is my favourite chapter," she says. "Each time I read it, I can see the people, smell the lake and hear the crackle of the bonfires we used to sit around. I can recall the laughter, the stories and the good times we used to have. Oh, I guess people around here still have good times, but life seems to be so rushed."

I read her introduction and am caught up immediately. "I love how she begins: *A story stranger than fiction is our heritage. It tells of a people who were as free as the air they breathed, who surrendered the greater part of their possessions for an annuity. Tracts of land which were of little use, except as a place to hunt, were purchased for them. Our ancestors acquiesced cheerfully in the belief that they could hunt where and when they wished "as long as the grass grows and the water runs" so ran the agreement signed by Indian chiefs and representatives of His Majesty's Government. This was the law and promise which our ancestors deemed invulnerable as the laws of the Medes and Persians, but which later proved to be only a scrap of paper. This work has been collected and compiled so that future generations may read the story of their origin, and that a better understanding may exist between us and our white brethren.*

*"So, 'we who sat in darkness have seen a great light,' and have emerged from a pagan state to become Christianized, have brought with us our culture, a charm and chivalry, and also a sense of humour which could laugh at adversity and poverty. May we give thanks, first of all, to the Giver of all good gifts, and bow in veneration before the early missionaries who braved the terrors of the forest to bring "Tidings of Great Joy". And last, but not least, to our own forefathers, who never failed to give thanks to "Manitou", the Great Spirit. An unconquered people, who preferred peace to war; and whose prayer was "O God, may I never judge another until I have walked at least two weeks in his moccasins." May we, who have not the ears of our forefathers, pay a tribute to Rice Lake,*

which gives life and sustenance to man, bird and beast. May it always look out on a world of Peace and Harmony, and flow on, ad infinitum."

What a wonderful tribute to a body of water that many of us take for granted. I continue leafing through the manuscript, skimming the contents, until I come to Life on the Lake, and read it to Gate-gan who's settled back on her pillows once again.

## LIFE ON THE LAKE
by Mary Jane Muskratte Simpson

Circa 1905

...Rice Lake flows diagonally, separating the counties of Northumberland and Durham, and derived its name from the abundance of wild black rice which grew in the shallow parts of the lake. It is 28 miles long, with an average width of three miles. Tributaries are the Otonabee and Indian rivers; it empties into the Trent River near Hastings. There are 27 islands of which Long Island, near Bewdley, is the largest, containing about 200 acres. The smallest is Little Grape Island at the head of the lake that is about 25 by 30 feet, on which grows a lone gooseberry bush....

Hiawatha is a Reserve of the Chippewa on the north shore of Rice Lake, and on the south shore are the Chippewa of Alderville [Chippewa and Ojibway are the same peoples]. Before the days of railways and good roads water was the main route of travel. Large side-wheeled steamers plied between Hastings on the Trent and Peterborough on the Otonabee, and carried passengers and freight between various points where the government had built wharves. Huge flatboats or scows were snubbed alongside or towed behind these boats, and carried freight, wood and cattle.

Some of the earliest boats on the lake were the City of Peterborough, a side-wheeler; the Rainbow, owned by Frank Burnet of Birdsalls; The Beaver, Tom Harris of Gore's Landing; the Monarch, the North Star, the Geneva, Golden Eye, and the Forest City. Many of these were piloted by members of the Harris family of Gore's Landing. Smaller steamers were owned and operated: the Firefly by Zack White, and one by James Wedlock of South Monaghan.

The social life of the surrounding district centred about the lake. Boats were chartered and picnics were held at Hiawatha on Dominion Day each year; and farmers' picnics were held at Jubilee Point at the mouth of the Otonabee River and Idyl Wyld, two miles east of Harwood. On the inevitable scow in tow, square dancing was enjoyed by the younger folk to the music of Albert Crowe's violin.

**The Eva** circa 1905

## The Rainbow
First constructed in 1898, later refurbished. Photo circa 1905

Canoe races and baseball games were popular sources of entertainment; moonlight excursions were also very popular. Albert Steele, who resided near Harwood, would rent a boat, usually The Rainbow. It picked up passengers at different government wharves and took them to Idyl Wyld, and some years to Jubilee Point. Dances were held at an outside pavilion with either Enock or Albert Crowe playing the violin...passengers danced on rough pine floors; the dancers of that day did not demand polished hardwood floors. Square dances were more in vogue then. The orchestra consisted of a violin and someone usually Tom Johnson of Harwood or Fred Kyle of Otonabee chording on a reed organ.

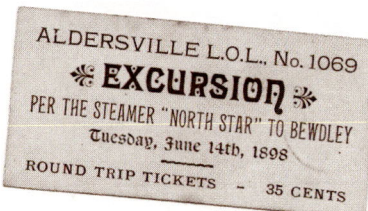

When I think of the jags I've been to at Vimy Ridge, I think of boom-boxes and what Gate-gan calls 'the infernal racket' of the music we play on them. It's hard for me to picture Mary Jane Muskratte Simpson's recollections, but the photographs are here to prove it. She mentions in her manuscript that a man named Samson Comego, at the turn of the century, did much to promote the cultural life of the community, organizing a brass band. And that he was succeeded by Samuel Blaker. She adds that Peter Crowe was also a renowned music teacher, and that he formed singing classes and taught sight-reading. He, along with his family, formed a famous concert troupe.

"Charlotte Crowe was Professor Peter Crowe's second wife," Gate-gan tells me as we are looking at a poster advertising one of Peter's concerts. "She was a very good singer, and a contemporary of the poet Pauline Johnson, with whom she used to perform on stage in Toronto. I was at Charlotte Crowe's 110th birthday in 1972. She was born January 18, 1862. She and Peter had six children, one of whom was Borden Crowe. Imagine, she lived to see 37 grandchildren, 103 great grandchildren, and 55 great-great grandchildren. She lived here on the reserve until she was 99, when she moved to the Golden Plough Lodge. That's where her birthday party was. She still sang with a strong voice and still insisted on three meals a day, right until her final day. She sang so well the residents taped her and she was featured in Christmas concerts. On her 110th birthday she sang 'Put On Your Old Grey Bonnet' for all to hear. Peter would have been proud of her."

Peter Crowe centre
Circa 1915

The brass bands at Alderville and Curve Lake toured but were always willing to assist in local gatherings. Watch-meetings were held on New Year's Eve in the Methodist church, which would start with a service by the local missionary. Then at the stroke of 12 midnight the band would play "Roll Round With the Year" MJMS    Photo circa 1920

Jam Session at Vimy Ridge circa 1930

The main event of the year was the July 1st picnic at Hiawatha, attended by hundreds who came mostly by steamboats: The City of Peterborough brought passengers from Peterborough and points along the Otonabee River. The Geneva, from Gore's Landing brought passengers from Gore's Landing and Harwood. The Rainbow brought passengers from Keene, Dunettes' and Robins' landings. And a smaller steamboat owned by James Wedlock came from Monaghan. The people from Otonabee came in carriages and brought full lunch baskets.

The little girls wore white cotton dresses, and long pigtails. The small boys wore knee pants; the women wore embroidered white blouses or waists as they were called, and dark ankle-length skirts. The men wore their hair parted in the centre; all wore moustaches and the elite wore narrow-brimmed hats called cadies that had hard crowns.

Booths were operated on the grounds; before the days of bottled pop and ice cream cones, there were huge milk cans of lemonade and homemade ice cream.

The canoe races which were keenly contested had entries from Alderville, Curve Lake which was then called Chemong, and Hiawatha. Alfred Crowe was the best paddler from Hiawatha; Zack Smoke from Alderville and the Taylor brothers from Chemong. No Henley Regatta was ever watched with more interest; so high did the feeling run that they usually ended up in a fight.

Oblivious to the sports, the young folk danced the afternoon away on the scows attached to the boats. They were flat-bottomed vessels with railings and roofs; the owners swept the floors clean and hired a fiddler– usually Albert Crowe of Alderville, a genial fellow, always ready to promote harmony and good fellowship.

All too soon, the day would end and the Union Jack which fluttered so proudly in the breeze would be taken down. The people would go to the boats, some to hitch up horses, content with the enjoyment of meeting with old friends, on the whole, a well-behaved people in those days, when people had to make their own amusement.

Marsden Reunion circa 1920

I can't help but think that I am looking at an impressionist painting, Renoir's idea of what Alderville looked like in the early 1900s. Though I can't recognize a soul in the photograph, the leisurely feeling of the day is certainly captured in the posture of the people there. The fence in the background suggests they were at Vimy, but Mary Jane describes a similar event in another popular location:

*A unique picnic was held each year in September on Sugar Island, owned by the Alderville people, many of whom camped there during the autumn to harvest wild rice. Tables were erected, and meals were served to the public. Special items on the menu were wild black duck, fish and wild rice pudding. Frank Joblin, missionary at Alderville, visited the island each Sunday, bringing services to his congregation.*

Christmas and New Year's were, with the Ojibways, occasions of much merriment. The village of Alderville is on one side of the lake, and that of Hiawatha opposite. The distance between them is about seven miles. One chief would order his villagers to give a dinner to the other reservation members on Christmas, and they in return, gave a dinner on New Year's Day.

When the Alderville people were nearing Hiawatha, they were met by the people of Hiawatha, by the chiefs and principal men. The joyous notes of the Alderville Brass Band could be heard before they rounded Paudash Point; they were escorted to the community hall where a sumptuous feast was prepared.

Norma (left) & Aunt Minnie
Beaver circa 1940

*In the winter seasons, sleigh-rides were popular and visits to neighbouring reservations, in large bodies, were quite frequent. In later years, at the turn of the century, sleigh-loads from Alderville would journey to Curve Lake, crossing Rice Lake, up the Indian River to Keene, through Peterborough. A stop for dinner would be made, and in some cases, they would have liquid refreshments, or as the earlier Indians termed it, "Englishman's tea". The trip would be resumed, over ice and roads, following the route of the crow. Loose straw would have been thrown on the bottom of the sleigh.*

    The men would wear coonskin coats; the women, before the days of long coats, would wear a three-quarter coat, with a warm skirt , and a multiplicity of petticoats.

    Much merriment was enjoyed on these trips, jokes and singsongs, journeying to these "tea-meetings".

    The supper would be followed by a concert, great latent was observed, in dialogues, group singing: harmonized, solos and duets, while the repartee of the M.C. kept everyone in good humour.

    The Alderville group, in turn, would sponsor an oyster supper sponsored by the executive of the brass band, alternately with the members of the Loyal Orange Lodge No. 1069. Similar oyster-suppers were held in Hiawatha, usually January in one place, February in Alderville, and the last in March, back at Hiawatha.  These suppers would be followed by a concert, highlighted by selections by the brass band. In points of merit, these concerts surpassed any modern shows that are seen now on television.

*Another interesting feature was a popular girl contest. One from each reserve was chosen. Men would pass the hat for a girl from their reserve. Whichever candidate had the most money would be the winner of a parlour lamp or a fruitcake.*

"That's where this old lamp came from," Gate-gan says, flicking the fringe on the chintz-covered shade. " Imagine. Me, of all people."

"I certainly can, and you have photographs to prove it, Gate-gan," I say to assure her, though I'm sure she needs none–if she is even listening. I sense she's remembering the good times she had as a younger woman.

"Bob Marsden once told me about his parents, Norman and Sarah, one New Year's Eve when they had gone over to Hiawatha for a party," said Gate-gan, fingering the tassels on the lamp shade. "At the stroke of midnight, blasts from shotguns could be heard clear across the lake, in unison with shots from our own boys' guns here in the Village. I don't know where that tradition originated, but shooting-in the new year has gone on for as long as I can remember. Anyway, the full moon had lit Norman and Sarah's journey across the lake to Hiawatha, but when they'd left to go back home in the wee hours of the new year, it was snowing so hard they couldn't see a foot in front of them. So they covered themselves in their fur robes, slackened the reins and let the horses take them home with no guidance or direction from Norman, whatsoever. Smart creatures, horses. Took them right to their front door."

I'm still back at the New Year's oyster supper, salivating. It is past noon, and just looking at my watch makes the juices in my stomach growl with anticipation. "How about a bite to eat, Gate-gan? I'm feeling kind of gaunt."

"How about smoked oysters on toast?" Gate-gan stretches and stands up.

"Perfect. I'll make the tea." Gate-gan had taught us very early on that if tea was to be any good at all, it should be steeping the whole time you're eating. You could stand your spoon up in Gate-gan's tea–that's why I offered to make it this time. Gate-gan and I move well together in the kitchen, almost like we're dancing. And like a culinary duet, the four-slice toaster pops and the kettle whistles in unison, sounds that cue us for our next tasks.

"Alton Bigwin has told me about the pails of oysters his father James used to bring home after those oyster suppers. Shucked, they were, and in some sort of brine. We'll suffice with our little canned smoked oysters today."

When we sit down at the table, Gate-gan and I clasp hands and thank the Creator for the food we are about to eat.

"*Chi miigwech,*" we say as one.

"Are you going to take a nap this afternoon, Gate-gan?"

"No way," she replies, quickly and definitely. "Too much to do. Like that librarian's bumper sticker I once saw: 'So much to read; so little time.'"

Indeed. By the time we finish lunch, the sun has moved to the west side of the house and Gate-gan's room, shaded only by flimsy sheer curtains, is taking the brunt of the afternoon's rays, making her little room feel like an oven. We push the trunk onto a floor mat and slide the mat, with the trunk on it, out to the dining room.

"There," I say when we succeed in getting it there. "We can spread things out on the table and be more comfortable out here."

" We won't get through it all today, but at least we don't have to worry about putting everything away," Gate-gan says, pulling a chair beside mine.

# Fred Simpson
# Marathon Runner
# 1878–1945

As I reach into the trunk for the next pile of papers, I find a number of photos and paper on one of my personal heroes, Fred Simpson, an Olympic Marathon runner who competed early in the 20th century. In high school, my track and field coach had pictures of Fred Simpson and Albert Smoke in his office and always pointed to them as the stars of their day, the best role models we could ever have.

"There were no Nike endorsements in those days," Gate-gan says. " He had to get there on his own hook. But in Peterborough a Simpson Olympic Fund was set up. Their goal was to raise $250 –you'd probably add a couple of zeros to that today. On June 10th, the day before he was to set off, the Peterborough Examiner reported that contributions were coming in rapidly, and they obviously met their goal."

We're looking at a university paper written in 1989 by Dave Mowat, great-grandson of Fred Simpson, but before I start reading it, Gate-gan is laughing. I ask her what's so funny.

"Fred ran most everywhere," Gate-gan begins, when she's stopped laughing. "Once he was running along a road, and a driver stopped in his horse and buggy to ask if he wanted a ride." "No thanks," said Simpson, "I'm in a hurry."

# The Ojibway Thunderbolt: Fred Simpson

by Dave Mowat, great grandson. 1989

Fred Simpson was born in Alderville in 1878, of James Simpson and Mary Mitchell. His grandfather was John Simpson, one of the first Christianized Mississauga Indians from Grape Island. Fred married Susan Evelyn Muskrat from Hiawatha in Ashburnham–now Peterborough. They lived and raised their children at Hiawatha, across Rice Lake. According to son, Jack Simpson, born in 1900, their family came across the lake twice–once in the early 20s. Susan, better known as Granny, got homesick [so they returned] and came back in 1923 and settled. It was coming home for Fred.

Fred and Susan had eight children at Hiawatha: Jack, Mae, Lucy, Charlton, who died in infancy, Fred Herald Simpson [if his father had won the Hamilton Herald Road Race, he would have been named Hamilton Herald Simpson], Olive, Dan and Lawrence.

Fred started running in 1906 with the Peterborough Examiner backing him. He placed second in the premier Hamilton Road Race in 1907. At that point, trainer Dick Baker took him under his wing. Fred placed fourth in both provincial and national 1908 Olympic trials, assuring him a place on the team. Not even a full three years of training and running [and 28 years old].

The 1908 Marathon was the most dramatic in the history of the Olympics. Tom Longboat was the favourite, but he conked out at 19/26 miles, and stunned the world. Dorando Pietri came into the stadium, staggered and fell. He was helped up by British officials, and fell down a total of four times, when he was hauled over the finish line. Following was US runner, Johnny Hayes. Americans lodged a protest and won. Pietri was disqualified but given a medal by Queen Alexandria. Fred Simpson finished sixth, stunning the sports world with his blazing speed at the end of the race–enduring a remarkable heat wave that downed other runners, including the favourite, Tom Longboat.

After that race there evolved a running boom (1908-1912), and many [runners] turned professional, with promoters sponsoring them. Fred turned professional in 1909, with his first pro race at Buffalo. He raced at New York City's Madison Square

Gardens, at the Polo Grounds on Long Island, and in Chicago. During his pro career, he trained in Savannah, Georgia, and raced in Christian Island, Fort William (Thunder Bay), Toronto, Montreal, the entire circuit, making between $400–500 per race, depending on how he finished. Tom Longboat made $17,000 in three years of professional running, while school teachers earned $400 annually.

While Longboat encountered crooked promoters, Fred went alone, with a manager who treated him fairly. He seldom quit a race, but when he did, his "lazy Indian"-ness was used against him. Otherwise, he was a well-respected Methodist who neither smoked nor drank. He played violin and used to sing in the Hiawatha choir.

**Ojibway Thunderbolt Fred Simpson** is on the left, beside another Canadian runner, Freddie McCarthy, at Harrow-on-the-Hill, England, at the 17.5 mile mark (8.5 miles from finish line) in the 1908 Olympic Marathon

**Diploma of Merit** awarded to Fred Simpson following the 1908 Olympic Games in London

**Albert Smoke**, another sports hero, emerges in a great photograph and mention of him running in the Boston Marathon in 1922, finishing 26 miles in 2 hours, 22 minutes and 49 seconds.

"It's amazing that even with war going on, people like Albert were competing in sports, and that far away," I say.

"Sports activities are great for developing muscles as well as developing and implementing strategies," Gate-gan says, sounding like an authority on the subject. "Mary Jane has written a bit on some of the sports that originated with our people."

In the realm of sport the Indian has always excelled. In the early days, the Chippewas had to provide their own amusement and recreation. A sort of football with both men and women taking part was enjoyed by the spectators too old or too young to take part.

The game of lacrosse, still popular among all nations, originated with the Indian nations. Hogball, a forerunner of baseball, was also played.

The two Hogball captains had a novel way of choosing sides: one captain threw a bat, similar to a baseball bat to the other captain who hung onto the bat where he caught it, and closing his hand around it, the other captain put his hand over; whichever hand reached the top first had the first choice of choosing players. Two goals were made, a player from the side that was out tossed a ball to the one batting; the players that were "out" would try to hit the player as he ran to the other goal after batting. When any of the runners were hit with the ball, that side was out.

In the day when marathon racing was popular, Fred Simpson and Albert Smoke of Alderville, and Ben Howard of Hiawatha made great names in this most gruelling of all racing.

# War

Later that afternoon, I pull out a tattered copy of Forgotten Heroes, a large format paperback about Native involvement during wartime. Its cover is bound with two pieces of cardboard, held together with elastics, beneath which old photographs, some with accompanying articles, medals and ribbons are held. Folded in the centre of the book is an essay with my great-grandmother's name on it.

"I didn't know you were a writer, Gate-gan."

"Oh, I can write if I get worked up about something," she chuckles. "I used to cringe every time I saw that book, remembering how angry I'd been when I read it for the first time. It infuriated me so much that I started researching the issue of racism in recruitment for both world wars. I wrote this paper just before one Remembrance Day many years ago. I never tried to have it published, it was just something I had to get off my chest, and I am still satisfied with the effort." I hand her the essay.

"Would you please read it to me, Gate-gan?" She adjusts her glasses and clears her throat.

"*Miigwech* for asking me."

### The Changing Face of War

*When we look at the great number of names etched into the monument that stands at the five roads of Alderville First Nation in southern Ontario, doubtless our hearts swell with pride and gratitude for these men who fought in wartime. But few people are aware that when the Great War in Europe drew troops from Britain's colonies, it was a modern war: different in style and in the attitude toward the savage warrior who'd been so effective in defending the colonies a mere hundred years earlier.*

*According to Sgt. James W. Walker, in an article entitled "Race and Recruitment in WWI: Enlistment of Visible Minorities in the Canadian Expeditionary Force," he writes that early on, the Militia Council had prohibited Natives from fighting, arguing that the "Germans might refuse to extend them the privileges of civilized warfare." The stereotypical Indian had preceded them to Europe from Britain and the United States, where accounts of scalping and blood curdling war whoops embellished the war stories of pre-Confederation. Indeed, pioneers to Upper Canada, authors and sisters Susanna Moodie and Catherine Parr Traill wrote several books from which their British publishers had deleted chapters, wanting more adventure and drama—something to excite readers. Only recently has one of Moodie's books been republished to include chapters about her very positive relationships with the Native people that her original publisher had omitted.*

*World War I had been a white man's war; slaughtering the European enemy, also white, might whet the killing instinct of the identifiable races in question, and might ultimately backfire on the supremacists if the Natives were ever to get restless when they got home.*

*In August, 1914, Canada was awash with a wave of patriotism, accelerated by high unemployment. Twenty-five thousand volunteers enlisted, so recruiting could be selective according to race. While local militia officers were able to discriminate, to handpick their troops, and racial policy backed them up, some less visible Natives were able to "slip through, undetected."*

*But here too, policy changed. War was also a numbers game, and when troops were being killed in battle, more troops needed to be enlisted. Enter the visible minorities who started to be called for non-combative duties, or enlisted in separate units. In November, 1915, the 114th Battalion was formed, initially to enlist four companies of Brantford and area Indians, and soon Indians from other regiments were invited to transfer to "the Indian Unit."*

*Every province from Ontario west produced proposals to enlist Natives in segregated units, where under careful supervision of white officers, their "natural talents" as fighters and marksmen could best be utilized. By late 1915, a "patriotic phase" introduced a policy that would allow any patriotic individual or group to form a battalion.*

*On the first of January, 1916, Prime Minister Borden pledged 500,000 troops to Europe. Factoring-in casualty rates, this meant that 300,000 recruits were required annually. Were the Indians becoming more attractive—or less visible? The colour of blood was the same in the trenches, regardless of race. By summer, Indians, Blacks and Japanese were all accepted, at least in theory. In the same year, to garner votes in the December election, Borden passed the Military Voters Bill that allowed veteran Indians the vote—as status Indians, according to Mr. Gaffen, author of Forgotten Soldiers.*

*But the ever-present segregationist approach to putting battalions together, as well as reports of discrimination and bad treatment overseas, eventually deadened the enthusiastic youth who became reluctant to enlist. Industry was up; there was work at home. Why go to a foreign country to die? "*

*Enter Conscription, with the Military Service Act of 1917 that required all British subjects in Canada between the ages of 20–45 years, to enlist. Automatically exempt were all clergy, Mennonites and Doukabors. Treaty Indians had to register for exemption, according to Mr. Gaffen.*

*The "wards of the Government" responded vehemently against conscription. Still considered legal minors with no democratic voice in how Canada was governed, they were supposed to fight as equals with white Canadians? It didn't wash. Because of these limitations, Treaty Indians were exempted from combat duty by an Order In Council of January 17, 1918, and any of them who'd enlisted between the Military Service Act and the Order In Council, were eligible for discharge.*

*Native Indians who served were enfranchised by the War Time Elections Act—but only the individuals; their families continued to be partially Canadian citizens. Nevertheless, while in other parts of the country, Treaty Indians were meeting with discrimination, the Ojibways of Alderville, as one of our Native historians, Mary Jane Muskratte Simpson, writes, "enlisted almost to a man." And our monument is a testament to their involvement.*

"I had no idea, Gate-gan, I manage to sputter."

"I'm sure very few other people know either."

"Veterans don't talk much about what they went through. As I say, Katie, I needed to get it off my chest." Gate-gan's head droops.

Robert Franklin (who was married to Josephine Comego) was gassed in World War I. He returned and later died in hospital

"You must be exhausted, Gate-gan. We've spent the entire day here in the depths of this trunk." I offer my arm to her and escort her back to her room. "You have a nap while I make us some dinner."

She appeared to go out like the chintz-covered lamp next to her bed. I, on the other hand, was charged like a new battery. Delving into the past with Gate-gan who is such a knowledgeable guide, reading other people's work and seeing what was important to them, their perspective, their fond memories of days long ago—all of it is like nourishment for my soul.

Each piece is so precious, some of the photographs are tintype studio portraits of nattily dressed Indian families, some are of locals who were photographed by Roy Studio in Peterborough that produced and marketed the photographs as postcards. There were professionally photographed studio portraits and there were snapshots, piles of them. I could see the curatorial tasks ahead of me.

I would need to buy some photo albums or get some kind of storage system that was acid-free, to protect them from further deterioration, and start the process of organizing the photographs and text into chronological order. As spry as Gate-gan is, she is also almost 90 years old, and I understand her sense of urgency in passing these things along to me while her memory is still sound and she has the energy to share her knowledge with me.

We leave the trunk in the diningroom that night with stacks of photos and papers all over the table—unheard of if Mom were here. It's not that she's such a neat freak, but living harmoniously with six people in this not-so-spacious house means that some measures must be taken if we want to avoid chaos. Gate-gan must have been planning our time alone together. We could spread ourselves all over the place and luxuriate in our freedom. And we'd only just begun.

After Gate-gan's nap, we sit down to dinner in the kitchen and both of us are quiet.

"I seem to be digesting more than food this evening, Gate-gan."

"You've certainly devoured a lot of information today," she replies. "And brought out a lot of old memories for me."

"It feels like all of it is circling inside my brain on a loop."

"Let's take a break tonight and watch television. North of 60 is on."

That is one of our favourite shows that the whole family watches together. I know the rest of the family is watching it on a portable down at the cottage. Tonight, however, the program is merely a backdrop for my thoughts which are centred on the contents of the trunk.

Gate-gan and I drive into town the next morning and while I leave her at the supermarket to shop, I go to a photo shop and find some plastic sleeves for photographs and then to the stationery store to buy 10 binders in which to put the sleeved photographs once I've labelled them. By the time I finish my errands, Gate-gan is standing outside No Frills with several bags of groceries. I pull up beside her and she stows the bags in the backseat.

Stocked with provisions and my curatorial supplies, we drive back to Alderville, put on the kettle for tea, and metaphorically dive back into the trunk again.

Back row: 2nd from left: Ernie Crowe, 4th: Amos Marsden, 5th: Norman Marsden. Chief Moses Marsden, far right
Front row 2nd from left: Tom Marsden, 5th George Blaker Senior
Circa 1907

## Moses Marsden   1870-1968

    As I sip my tea, I sort through scads of photographs from both World War I and World War II and arrange them in an album. Front and centre is one of the Roy Studio postcards of the Alderville band. Gate-gan looks at it for a long time before she speaks.

    "The man in the bowler hat on the far right is Moses Marsden. He was born June 15, 1870, and was Chief here from 1903 until 1910. He gave an interview in 1968 that I've listened to, wherein he described his early work as a Native river driver, and this timber contract has him selling logs from Dunnet's Landing in 1924. Papers at the Public Archives in Ottawa list him as being enfranchised on August 20, 1909, but he argued that it was 1912, and I'd believe him ahead of some bureaucrat in Ottawa. And you'll see that some newspaper photographed him, claiming he was 103. Did the reporter get it wrong or was Moses pulling his leg? Anyway, he's a relative of ours through his marriage to Nellie Franklin. They had 13 children in all, but only nine survived.

"Moses enlisted in 1915 to fight in World War I and joined the 139th Battalion of Cobourg as a bandsman. A day before the battalion was ordered overseas, he and several other men were honorably discharged. Since he had been enfranchised, Moses and his family settled up in Lakefield in 1925. He was a master builder of log cabins, including one he built for a United States Secretary of State. From the 1930s through to 1960s, it was hard to find a newspaper around that didn't have one of his letters to the editor published in it. He gave his perspective on hunting and fishing laws and on treaties and surrenders that did not acknowledge compensation for enfranchised First Nations peoples who were not on the reserve at the time it was paid, but was a birthright to Indians born at Alderville, he claimed."

Model log home made by Moses Marsden

Using a slick at 86

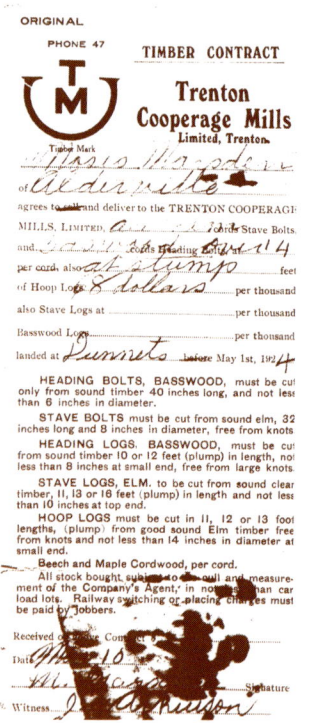

Timber contract 1924

"This death certificate is for the Robert Franklin who first had the general store at the five roads, later owned by Bob Marsden, then Sandercock's, and now Lloyd's," Gate-gan explains. "Moses would have been chief then, and would have signed the death certificate. So there. We have our own proof that he was still on the reserve, acting as chief in 1911, and didn't enfranchise until 1912, like he said."

## The Service

Circa 1917

"Allie Loukes used to say that many of the boys who enlisted thought they were going to play their way through the war. Didn't they get a big surprise?"

Circa 1917

# Norman Marsden
# 1881-1957

Gate-gan thumbs back to the group shot in front of the 139th Battalion crest and points to one of the men.

"That's Norman Marsden there. He served in the 139th Battalion in World War I. Then when WWII was declared, as veterans, he and Edward Beaver joined the Voluntary Service to guard German prisoners-of war. When he came back to the Village, he served as Alderville's Chief for 28 years."

Voluntary Service and King George VI medals

Northumberland 139th Overseas Battalion

## Alvin Hagar

Several photos of the same man emerge in a small stack. "Alvin Hagar," Gate-gan tells me. "Handsome man, isn't he?" I have to agree. Gate-gan points back to a man in a previous shot. "That's Alvin Hagar's father. He too was in the 139th Battalion in WWI."

"Alvin served in the Ordinance Corp in WWII. These are some of his buddies when they were overseas." Gate-gan shuffles through the photographs. "Then, after he was discharged from the war, he enlisted in the 48th Militia. And after that, he joined the Royal Regiment, and here you see him marching at the head of the parade. He told me he just liked being in the service," Gate-gan explains.

"Did you ever get a chance to speak to these men about discrimination?" I ask. Gate-gan smiles.

"The only discrimination Alvin ever told me about was one time when he was at a dance. The woman he was dancing with asked him if he'd been down south...he had such a good tan. He told her he hadn't been anywhere. That he was Native Canadian. The woman walked off the dance floor, and though Alvin saw her at other dances, he never spoke to her again."

Alvin Hagar
1939

Art Beaver  George Blaker  Alvin Hagar
Circa 1942

Lawson Chase (left), Wm Chubb,
Alvin Hagar 1939

# Reflections From Bob Marsden

# 1923–2001

Gate-gan looks at the photograph in my hand.
"Bob Marsden. Norman's son. We used to talk about the old days when the Village was more isolated and there were more people here–they didn't leave home. When the road from Cobourg to Hastings had troughs along the sides of the roads, to water the horses. His father farmed during the Depression, shipping livestock to Toronto. All the kids worked, and the operation wasn't as expensive as it would be today. They always had eggs and vegetables. He claimed there wasn't much money floating around, but he and his family always made it through.

"His Mom and Dad both spoke "Indian", as he called it, but they both stopped when he and the other kids came around. He said he was sorry that he hadn't learned to speak Ojibway."

His mother, Sarah, Mrs. Norman Marsden, turned the first sod for the monument, when Norman was Chief.

Bob fondly remembered oyster suppers. Oysters were bought in gallon pails in Cobourg. He used to reminisce about some of the tricks played on Hallowe'en, like putting buggies on barn roofs. And he remembered families getting along, helping each other. There were bees for cutting wood, and a lot of trading went on. Back in the 1920s, he recalled rice gathering on Rice Lake. They camped on Sugar Island. Back then, there weren't very many weeds.

"Bob was quite a bit younger than me, but I knew him. He was still attending Campbellford High School when he joined the army in World War II. He went off to do basic training in Brantford, then he shipped off to France in January, 1942. There were seven boys (and four girls) in the Marsden family: Hilton, Leslie, Bruce, Wallie, Norman, Verne and Bob. Brother Norman served, and he and Bob spent their leaves together. His other brothers, Leslie and Bruce, who had moved to the United States during the Depression, joined the US Army. Bruce's son, Butch, later served in Viet Nam."

"Did any women serve overseas, Gate-gan?"

"As I recall, Beatrice Smoke, Stephen Smoke's daughter, was the only woman to serve in either of the wars. Other women worked in factories in Toronto, on assembly lines that were making equipment used in the war effort, but the women didn't see combat. They didn't leave Canada.

" A lot of guys were out of work and they said going to war was a good way to make a living. The going rate was between $1.10 and $1.30 a day, plus clothing and board. Bob said everyone got more than their fill of mutton and brussel sprouts, and sausage that tasted like sawdust. Terrible. He said that most of the men didn't know just how tough it would be overseas. But I guess once they'd committed, they went ahead. They'd made that decision; and they couldn't turn back. But they weren't alone, and as Bob used to say, " you'd try to save someone." Overseas he met up with James Smoke, Albert Bigwin, and Raymond Blaker. Wouldn't that be something? That far away from home.

"Oh, Bob used to love the parcels he received from the Village. All the boys appreciated them, though some didn't make it through the mail. Hope Her Majesty's beggars enjoyed the fruitcakes they intercepted in the mail room. The boys would send gifts to us girls too: stockings. In those hard times, women used to paint their legs the colour of stockings. Good for dry weather, but on rainy days, the paint used to wash off. Wouldn't that make you feel cheap?" Gate-gan visibly darkens with embarrassment.

Gate-gan says that Bob never mentioned any discrimination against Natives either. "We were all the same," he used to say. But he also said that he thought there was more discrimination in the United States with the Whites against the Blacks.

" Bob used to say that the toughest part of the war was getting injured in 1944, and being shipped home," Gate-gan tells me. Still, he was given a pension of $37.50 per month, and attended a rehabilitation school on Gold Street in Toronto, where he finished high school and took up cabinet making. He became the first Native postal carrier, and during his time there three other Native people were hired. He worked for the Post Office in Toronto from 1950 until his health forced him to retire in 1974.

Bob Marsden (above) hosts a birthday party for Alvin Hagar in 1991, both seated at a picnic table that tips when Bob rises– and Alvin with it

# Bill Bigwin

# 1910–1991

"A hard time but a good time."

We are looking at a contemplative shot of a little old man Gate-gan tells me is Bill Bigwin.
"He was a bit older than me. I was closer to his sister, Lizzie. Boy, he came from a big family: there was Albert, Jim, Bill, Elmer (who died as a child), Marjorie, Mary, Phyllis, baby Ella, 'who died small', and Lizzie. When he was a young lad, there wasn't a lot to eat, nothing to eat at times, he told me. He said he always went to church when he was a child, and remembers Dodson as the best minister. He had no fondness for Joblin, the minister-teacher who used a pointer to prod his students. When he was an old man, Bill still had the scar of one prodding that had abscessed on his ribcage.
"He was 80 years old when I last talked to him," Gate-gan continues, " but he sure had vivid memories of the brief time he spent at Muncey Residential School when he was 12 years old, and overseas, when he served in World War II. He is one man who will tell you what institutions can do to a person. It was during Chief Ernie Crowe's term that Josh, Raymond and Mildred Blaker, plus Mary, Phyllis and Bill Bigwin were sent to the Muncey Residential School. Bill Coyle was the last Indian Agent he remembers and hated, because Coyle was Indian Agent when Bill was sent to Muncey. They were tough times for Bill, who didn't last long there before he jumped a train back to Hastings and walked home to Alderville.

"Bill had a connection with Curve Lake through his mother (Marie-"Gal" Taylor), and with Rama through his grandparents (John Bigwind), ties with more traditional Native communities. For many years, Bill and his sister, Elizabeth Crowe and brother, Jim Bigwin, were the only elders of Alderville who spoke their Ojibway language. Before they passed away, Bill and Lizzie had been happy to hear that the Ojibway language was to be taught at Roseneath Centennial School.

" 'The French, the Japanese, they all talk their own language, why don't we?' was one of Bill's rhetorical questions." Gate-gan sips her tea, tapping her finger gently on the porcelain.

"Bill served four years overseas in World War II, and saw a lot of action in France, and in Germany," she continues. "He used to tell about sitting in a pub in London, England, when in came his brother, Albert. And of hearing Albert's voice over a wireless radio, asking to speak to an Anishinabeg called Bill Bigwin. They'd spoken in Ojibway, of where they were going, Albert to Italy, Bill to France. Bill said it was a hard go but he always knew we were going to win the war. We were on the right side, he said. Oh, he had fond memories, but he said that the horrors of war were constantly with him, the smell of fresh blood, of bloating corpses, all too clear in his mind." Gate-gan looked away at some distant scene that seemed to make her face crumple with the emotional weight of it.

"But Bill never recalled any discrimination in the war either. The Indians were treated the same as the rest. One guy wasn't any better than the other, he used to say. But he often spoke of a racial incident that happened long ago, when they used to travel from Peterborough to Trenton on the waterway.

"Bill had offered to pilot a guy up to Peterborough, but the man said no. Bill asked him why and the man replied, 'because you're Indian.' Bill said fine and got the next ship that was going by and later that day they found the man piled up on the rocks. The guy Bill was with suggested they pull him off the rocks. 'Don't you touch him,' warned Bill, 'if that damn boat sinks, you're the goat. And it'll be your fault.'

"He loved the traditional drum though he claimed to have danced only once. He used to burn cedar on an electric element on his stove when it stormed, and when he was scared. He used to say, 'Don't burn it; pull it away before it burns. That smoke is for the Guy.' He burned sweetgrass during thunderstorms to give Him a smoke.

"Bill married Irene Beaver in the 1930s. He worked as a farmhand, as a fishing guide, and in later years, he worked in greenhouses in Clarkson. He used to talk about fishing through the ice on Rice Lake, and in 1990, the year before he died, in 1990, he'd been happy to hear that local Anishinabeg were allowed to fish legally on Rice Lake in the winter.

"For as rough a man as Bill appeared to be, he was very sensitive," Gate-gan smiles, her eyes glistening. " A couple of years before he died, he attended church and the presiding minister said it was a wonder the church didn't fall over when Bill walked in. Bill was so hurt that he walked away from the minister. People may have wondered why he did that, but I never questioned him for a moment: it hurt. And I always understood why he never went back. Still, I know that he thought about the Great Spirit and prayed every night on his own since that day he'd been insulted by a man of the cloth. During his final days in hospital, a nurse told me she had heard him singing in Ojibway late at night in his room.

"An old man once told Bill that he'd live a long time. He did: 80 years, but still not long enough," Gate-gan sighs.

"Long may his memory live," I say as I slide his photo into the album along with his compatriots.

When World War I was over, and all was said and done, Mary Simpson wrote about the war monument which I placed in the album along with photographs illustrating the war monument's construction.

## WAR MONUMENT
### by Mary Jane Muskratte Simpson

  The Indian has always been deeply religious. Long before the coming of the white man he sensed the presence of the Great Spirit. So that when the conflict and upheaval of 1914 came, they enlisted almost to a man, joining the ranks of their white brothers in the common cause: Freedom, which has been the goal of all, down through the centuries.
  In 1927 a committee was formed under the leadership of Indian Agent W. R. Coyle, and the Rev. Harold Wilding, and a large monument was erected on the Alderville village square, on land donated by William Loukes. This imposing monument, approximately 50 feet high, stands at the centre of the reserve on Highway 45 at an intersection where five roads meet; and across from the old post office where William Loukes was postmaster for years before the day of rural mail delivery. Three upright columns represent the Trinity. These are set on an octagonal concrete base, and surmounted by a large square block laid perpendicular, representing the Four Square. It is enclosed with a chain of cast iron joined to nine concrete blocks, in memory of the nine men who were killed overseas; and 35 links of chain stand for the 35 men who enlisted.
  Melody Crowe and Arlene Beaver learned more about the monument when they interviewed many members of the community in 1981. The first sod was turned by Mrs. Norman Marsden on August 21,1927. The monument was constructed by Alf McKeel and Son of Campbellford, who supplied the design and donated the materials for the project...the actual building of the memorial was carried out by the men of the band, some of whom were also employees of McKeel and Son.
  The monument was built in much the same way as construction during Biblical times, with the concrete being formed and then carried in relays, up a set of stairs, like the Pyramids. The cube of concrete on the top is quite secure, with three steel

rods embedded in the concrete for support. The building of the memorial was an impressive effort in cooperation. The Cobourg Marble Company contributed the marble tablet and members of Alderville First Nation brought or bought the material and laboured voluntarily, to keep the cost as low as possible. Loads of stone were hauled from a local field by horses and carts. The footing at the base is more than 10 feet deep because of the size and weight of the monument–Four hundred and sixty-eight tons of concrete went into the structure. The cube was formed and built on the very top of the monument.

Mr. McKeel, who refused any payment for the construction and design of the monument, was usually up at 4 am. to begin work. The monument was unveiled September 25,1927, with an attendance of 5,000 people at a dedication service. Mr. McKeel enjoyed a supper prepared in his honour by the women of the reserve. He was also presented with a gold watch from members of the band and council.

Grampa Bob Marsden (left)
& Mr. McKeel
Circa late 1920s

Shirley and brother Kingsley Crowe at foot of construction in 1927

Sarah and Chief Norman Marsden. Sarah turned the first sod when construction on the monument began.
Photo circa 1950s

# Sports and the Dirty Thirties

Gate-gan has positioned some sports photographs that show how many young men managed to get through the Dirty Thirties in relatively good spirits. Moses Marsden's liniment recipe makes me smile. I know people who own race horses and they use a similar concoction. The same recipe, but they also leave the shells on the eggs—which dissolve and thicken the liniment, but Moses didn't mention this in his recipe.

"There's the guy who made the steel-tipped paddles I told you about when we were talking about the springtime trips across the lake to the sugar bush," she says pointing to the great shot of the goalie, Everett Simpson.

MOSES MARSDEN'S LINIMENT

4 ounces ammonia
4 ounces turpentine
4 ounces vinegar
2 eggs
1 large cake of camphor
Mix well and shake well.
Rub on muscles for all pains and sprains.

In hockey, Everett Simpson was goalkeeper for the Cobourg Junior team and later for the Al Siratt Grotto team in Cleveland in the 1930s

In 1931, Ernest Crowe, manager of a hardball team, brought his men to victory over every team in the district, winning both the East and West Northumberland County championships, and the silver cup. MJMS

**1931 Northumberland County Hardball Champions**
Back Row: J. Bigwin, B. Marsden, A. Loukes, J. Loukes, G. Smoke, E. Marsden, W. Chubb, J. Simpson, W. Smoke
Front Row: F. Simpson, A Marsden, E. Crowe, A. Beaver, W. Crowe

John Wesley Beaver
Late 1930s

"I've tried to find a photograph of Jack with his gloves on," Gate-gan says, shuffling through a stack of photos. "He won the middleweight boxing title at Queen's University while he was studying there after the war, you know, but nobody seems to have a photo. You can imagine what he looked like though, from this photograph."

# Alderville's 100th Anniversary: 1937

We come to Alderville's 100th anniversary of settlement as a community, another event that occurred during the Depression.

"It's like Mary Jane Muskrat Simpson wrote, that we could smile in the face of adversity, or words to that effect," I say to Gate-gan before I notice that she's closed her eyes.

I study a school portrait taken during the 1937 Centennial celebration to see if I can identify people without Gate-gan's help.

Teacher John Loukes is on the right. Elder George Beaver is on the left. George used to make magazine racks that he'd decorate with symbols burned or carved into the wood. Not too long ago, one sold on E-Bay for $585 US. Two of them have been sold to the Museum of Civilization in Ottawa–though the information they have on his age is wrong, according to Gate-gan. No doubt she'll mention it later.

# CENTENNIAL CELEBRATIONS

by Mary Jane Muskratte Simpson

*The Indians of Alnwick township marked their Centennial October 10 and 11, 1937, commemorating their migration to Alderville from Grape Island in the Bay of Quinte.*

*Two special services of commemoration were held; the chalice used was originally presented to the Rev. John Sunday by Queen Victoria. The Rev. L. W. Scott presided, and Dr. F. Stephenson of the Home Mission Board of Toronto was guest speaker. Psalm 103, on which Elder Case preached at the London Conference in 1855, was the chosen text. A memorial service was held at the monument to Elder Case and John Sunday in the cemetery; a wreath was placed by Robert Marsden, who, in 1855, had attended the funeral of Elder Case. Mr. William Macklin presented an oil lamp which had belonged to and been used by Elder Case, and it is planned that this historic lamp will be wired and used in the church.*

**"Harvest Home"** Gifts from Mother Earth adorn the altar beneath the electrified lamp at harvest time. Thorn apples were threaded and hung around the church

Mary Ann Black, George Beaver and Ellen Loukes

A pageant was held, "One Hundred Years of Progress"; a musket over one hundred years old was carried by Mr. George Beaver, the oldest in the parade. A miniature replica of the church, complete even to the weather vane, was built by Mr. Everett Simpson and Mr. Clifford Smoke, and attracted much interest. A large birthday cake, trimmed with tiny flags and canoes of tinsel, was cut by Mrs. William Loukes, 87, the oldest lady resident, and sold by Mrs. Delany and Mrs. Fred Simpson. Mr. Johnson Paudash of Hiawatha, grandson of Chief George Potash, who was pilot of the boat which carried the Prince of Wales across Rice Lake in 1860, spoke of the traditions of the people of Alderville. While historians write of three tribes he felt there were, in reality, only two: the Iroquois, and two branches of the Algonquins, one part of whom had been named "Hurons" by the early Jesuit missionaries. From this branch stemmed the Mississaugas, who traditionally came from the south centuries ago, and were found by the Jesuits in Algoma. In 1615 Champlain accompanied them on a raid from Lake Couchiching to the Talbot River, Balsam Lake, through the Kawarthas and Rice Lake, to the Iroquoian territory south of Lake Ontario. MJMS

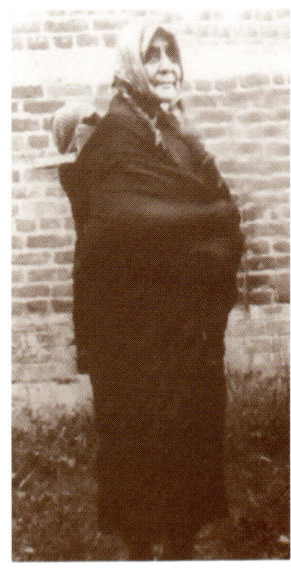

Mary Ann Black with bundle-board

# Hunting & Gathering

Berry Picking in Clarkson 1930s

The next photograph I come upon is entitled Berry Picking In Clarkson. "Clarkson?" I repeat to Gate-gan who has roused from her cat nap. "I know that's a city or town near Toronto, but what's this all about?" Gate-gan looks fondly at the photograph.

"Elmer Marsden will tell you that from when he was 12 or 13, in the late 1930s, he and many members of the community, young and old alike, spent the growing season working on farms outside of Toronto, in Clarkson, and at the MacMillan's in Oakville, often for $1.00 a day or sometimes 25 cents an hour. Elmer and Neil Crowe, along with many other people from Alderville, would pile into the back of a truck and be delivered to their summer jobs. They stayed in cabins or tents there and would pick strawberries, the first fruits of the season, and continue picking crops until the fall when the root crops were dug and the apples were harvested. Elmer says even though the amount they were paid was meager, money was hard to come by anywhere in those days, and they'd make enough to live through the winter. I must have been home having babies then. In later years, in the 50s and 60s, when farmers in Northumberland County discovered that their sandy soil was perfect for growing tobacco, people from the Village got jobs cultivating, and following the tobacco plants through their various stages of growing, harvesting, drying and shipping. I managed to miss out on that backbreaking work too," Gate-gan smiles and leans over me to look at photographs that have surfaced.

Harvest and Horseshoes circa 1930s

Chris Marsden, standing, his wife, Lily seated to his far-right
Circa 1890

Tom Salt & William Loukes
Circa 1890

Alf Simpson filleting fish 1908

"Alf was like our own personal Farmers' Almanac," Gate-gan tells me. "At the age of 84, he predicted that the winter was going to be 'open'. He knew this because he'd seen snakes, some birds hadn't left, and squirrels were not as active. Also, he'd seen sprouts on a lilac in December, and that meant an 'open winter' would follow. He was referring to Rice Lake, that it wouldn't freeze. He didn't bother with OFF or any of the commercial products used for keeping mosquitoes and black-flies away," Gate-gan smiled, remembering. "He rubbed on lard and coal oil instead," she said, pointing to the photo of Alf filleting fish.

"I can't help thinking that the men must have loved the kind of work they were able to do, like guiding fishermen," I say to Gate-gan. "I've heard about some of their shore dinners, making scone and frying up some of their day's catch."

"Sugar Island is all right in the daytime," says Gate-gan. "But I wouldn't want to spend a night there. I've heard from many boys who've gone over there to hunt, setting up the night before, and hearing movement around them. The place is filled with spirits from who knows what period of time."

Fred Simpson seated in front of fire on Sugar Island in late 1920s

"Women like Mae Black enjoyed keeping a lodge too," I say to change the subject when I find her photograph.

"It was hard work but she was able to hire women to help her," Gate-gan explains. "She also had a lodge at Hiawatha and employed many of the boys from the Village including Zack, Moses, and Steve Smoke, to work as guides for her fishermen guests."

Mae Black at Locust Lodge in the 1920s

# Wild Rice

Alfred Crowe (left) and Pook Anderson gathering wild rice on Rice Lake 1907

Finally, just like Gate-gan said I would, I come to the remaining transcript pages of Rick and Jeff Beaver's recollections of the wild rice harvests more than 40 years ago, when many people travelled to Ardoch to gather rice.

In those days, everyone needed to be involved in order to get things done—fishing, ricing, hunting. Many followed these traditional pursuits, attempting to be self-sufficient, and like-minded individuals sought their own kind in these efforts. They used to live off the land, camp together. People with jobs took time off work, the whole family would arrive in early September and go to Harold Perry's campground in Ardoch. Harold's brother, Neil, his sister, all of them were there.

Jeff remembers "going back to Ardoch with Grampa Ross 40 years ago. The roads were unbelievably bad. Grampa Ross was born there in a one-room cabin on a hill where lilacs and old apple trees still grow but the cabin has since rotted into the earth. Grampa Ross used to swim up the river to school. He married Bertie who was from Alderville, so he was here a lot, but he worked in Ardoch."

Rick remembers hearing about his dad harvesting 10 to 15 burlap bags of rice with Grampa Ross. They camped right there. When Rick lived in Deep River, he remembers his Grampa Ross dancing rice up there too. Deep River still had lots of rice because the area hadn't been developed and there was little alteration in water quality.

Rick remembers going to Ardoch when he was younger than 10 years old. "Our family spent a lot of time off reserve, but we always harvested rice. When I played baseball, I always took rice pudding to games for a snack. An old Ojibway staple. We always had it...never were without it."

Their grandfather, Amos Marsden, drove a Model T Ford, and on one trip from Alderville to Ardoch, he had 18 flat tires. The tires were like a toad's back, mottled with patches, according to Rick. The old hills were so steep, his car had more power in reverse, so he would back up the hills.

Rick's Aunt Carolyn and Uncle Jim Powers often arrived at the Beaver house when they lived in Barrie and 'riced' at Little Lake. "We didn't have a pot to parch the rice in, Rick says in the transcript, " so we used a GSW wash tub and canted it on a slant. Sometimes Jim would sneak down to the laundromat to parch the rice in pillow cases in the dryer. Can you imagine what would happen to the worms?"

Henry Comego with his rice sticks, waiting for his ricing partner circa 1930

Alf Simpson (left) and Wilfred Sunday drying wild rice in 1908

Rick and Jeff learned to rice by watching everybody else. They explain the process. First, before gathering, be sure to clean out the canoe to avoid sand getting into the rice. There's nothing worse than eating gritty rice.

The person at the bow of the canoe slowly paddles, or poles, through the rice beds. The person at the stern holds a tapered stick in each hand and pulls rice stalks over the gunnels of the canoe with one stick, and with the other, taps the ripe grains from the stalk (only the ripe will drop off the stalk), to fall into the canoe. Ricers have their own style of tapping—Jeff's is a double tap. In a good harvest, the showering of rice that falls on the bottom of the canoe soon accumulates, and nearly reaches the gunnels, yielding a few bags of unprocessed wet rice.

The next step is to bag it up in burlap or feed-store bags. If there are worms, and there will be, the bags are soaked in the lake for a couple of days. Rice worms become moths like Linden Loopers. Minnows will wait outside the bag and grab the worms as they try to slither out. If you plan to transplant the rice, it must be soaked too.

Spread the rice on canvas tarps to dry in the sun. Cattail mats were used in the old days. Then, like they know it is their harvest season too, wasps and crickets arrive to eat the rest of the worms.

While it is drying two to four days, the rice is turned over, and raked. Its texture feels slippery when it's nice and dry.

Parching wild rice (unknown) circa 1907

To parch the rice a large cast iron pot is needed (large enough to stand up in). Build a low fire and put the pot over it with the rice in it. Stir the rice with a paddle, turning it, watching the steam come off the rice which will turn a golden brown as it dries. Women traditionally took care of parching. Rice keeps better when dry and after parching, the grains swell. It keeps for years without dancing it.

Alf Simpson dancing rice
Circa 1907

Getting Ready to Winnow
(unknown) circa 1907

Dancing the rice loosens the hulls from the grains. Some people like to dance the first batch and leave in the hulls from the first dance, so the grains won't break. Traditionally, dancers would wear new moccasins -that would depend on the family's budget. We wear rubber boots.

When dancing the rice, make sure your (rubber) boots are clean. Rick says that traditionally, fire pits were built under a mat of deer skin. Dancing meant tromping around on the hide covered in rice, then winnowing –letting the wind blow the hulls away and the rice grains fell into baskets. The finished rice is stored in glass sealers or Tupperware today. Traditionally, the women made birch bark boxes to store it in.

Both Jeff and Rick say they learned a lot about cooking from their grandmother, and how not to cook rice from their grandfather. "Grandpa Amos once prepared a turkey when his wife, Mabel, wasn't around. He fired dry rice into the turkey...and while it was cooking in the oven, the rice puffed out through the skin of the turkey and looked like porcupine's quills."

Rick quotes from Melody Crowe and Arlene Beaver's research in 1981, that hunting and gathering served many harvesters an income as well as providing sustenance: From 1919 until 1948, Stanley Taylor, a storeowner in Keene, on the north shore of Rice Lake, bought unprocessed rice from Alderville and Hiawatha harvesters, trading them commodities for the rice. When he retired from the store he continued to buy rice–from 3,000 to 9,000 pounds a year. He advertised the seed for sale in sportsmen's magazines for spring propagation. He stored the rice in a spring-fed well at the grist mill in Keene, and as orders came in, he packed the damp, sprouting rice in moss-lined boxes and shipped them all over the world. Melody writes that when rice was abundant on Rice Lake, two men could harvest 300 pounds a day, and might work over the rice bed up to four times as the rice ripened.

Today, the lake doesn't move and as a result, doesn't have oxygen. Rice likes creeks, rapids, lakes. It doesn't like traffic to disturb it at the floating leaf stage, after which it bolts, or forms the stalk. Today, it gets drowned by boats, by carp and by the raising of the water levels when the Trent Canal System was built. On Rice Lake, the rice started to die out by the 1930s. Rick's mother, Marjory, remembers as a child being picked up by her father Amos, in a canoe and they would paddle (or pole) through rice to Sugar Island where they'd stay for the weekend. It was probably the social center for the season since it was one of the largest beds in the country. Now most young people under 25 don't go ricing...and if they do, they only gather rice for a few hours – but they sure like to eat it!

"These recipes look familiar, Gate-gan," I mention as I look at the ingredients.

"Yes, well, I've adapted them over the years," says Gate-gan. "We didn't have all the fancy ingredients in the old days."

## Wild Rice Pudding

1 cup uncooked wild rice  
½ cup sugar or maple syrup  
½ tsp. nutmeg  
2 cups milk  
2 eggs  
1 tsp. vanilla  

Soak rice overnight, drain, rinse and drain again. Preheat oven to 350 F. Put rice into a large ovenproof dish that has been greased. In a bowl, mix milk, sugar, eggs, sugar, vanilla and nutmeg. Pour over rice and mix well. Bake in oven for 1 hour or until a clean knife can be inserted into pudding and removed with a clear liquid on it–not milky."

## Wild Rice Stuffing

1 c. uncooked rice  
2 c. water  
½ tsp. salt  
2 tbsp. butter  
1 tsp. sage  
1 onion  
2 stalks celery  
12 water chestnuts  
6 dried prunes or apricots  
½ tsp. black pepper  

Depending on the size of the bird to be stuffed, remember that 1 cup of uncooked wild rice will yield 3 cups when cooked. Drain and rinse wild rice that has soaked overnight. Place in a saucepan with water and salt. Possibly use water that giblets have boiled in, or potato water. Cover and simmer after coming to a boil, for 20 minutes. While rice is cooking, chop onion, celery, water chestnuts and prunes. Saute onions and celery in butter. When rice is cooked, remove from heat and add chopped ingredients, sage and pepper. Mix well. Stuff into fowl, closing the opening with thread or skewers. Roast fowl for 20 minutes per pound.

# Borden Crowe
# 1905-1985

"That's Borden Crowe when he was a young boy. Peter's son. It was hard to know where to put Borden, he figures in so many aspects of village life throughout the years. He was born in 1905, married in 1925 and he and Lucy (nee Simpson) had 10 children. He was chief of the band for two consecutive terms from 1963 to 1967 and administrator for many years. But he was known as a great marksman, a talented musician and a trapper. He and his son Larry placed first and second in a provincial rifle meet and the following year did the same at the Dominion Rifle Competition. Later on, you'll see his son Merrill with all kinds of trophies for his car racing. Merrill also got his prizewinning knack of pitching horseshoes from Borden.

Borden Crowe (above) 1919 and by his canoe circa 1930

"His granddaughter, Melody, spent a lot of time with him. She says she learned a lot of things from him. He was swift on his feet and taught his children and grandchildren to walk quietly in the woods." Circa 1950

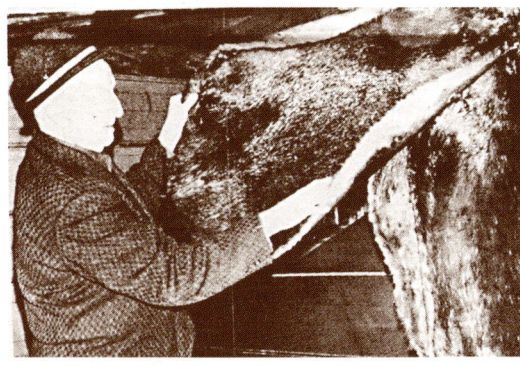

Borden examines a beaver pelt 1975

Fox pelts

**Borden and Lucy Crowe's children circa 1948**

Back row left, Roger, Sheila, Glen, Neil, Shirley and Kingsley.
Front row left: Dixie, Merrill, Larry and Wally

"Borden and his family lived in that big white house on Highway 45, just down from where his son Glen lives now. Glen got into trapping like Borden and Glen's son, Garry, got it naturally. They've all got camps down at Bradley Bay on the way to Stirling. An ancestral trapping locale that is like our own everglades. A pretty lively place.

"He died at the end of March in 1985. Boy what a day. On the day of his funeral, the church was full and the wind was so strong we all thought the windows would blow out. Then, boof, the ice pellets started. Before the day was over, more than four trees were uprooted in Borden's yard."

# Trapping

Garry Crowe's first camp at Bradley Bay
Photo taken 1990

I read a short interview with Garry Crowe about his trapping experiences in Bradley Bay and the folklore that surrounds the place. He said that up until the late 1970s, early 80s, Merne Brown (another cigar smoker) was the local fur trader in Roseneath, the hamlet north of Alderville, where many trappers sold their pelts to Brown for his furrier market in Toronto. Garry and his uncle Jack, aka "Dad" Simpson, were two of his customers. When he was younger, Garry trapped with his Uncle Jack, and in those days they often trapped on Hickory Island in Rice Lake.

"A man named Smith claimed he owned the island," said Garry, "but we trapped on it anyway and if Smith came, we'd fill our hip waders with what we'd trapped so he wouldn't take our animals."

In the spring and fall of each year since he was a boy, Garry Crowe trapped the waters around Bradley Bay for beaver, mink and muskrat. The lowest price he could ever remember getting for muskrats was 85 cents a pelt. The highest: $12 to $14. At the time of the interview in 1990, fur graders in North Bay were paying $3 to $4 per muskrat. Some beaver pelts he trapped had an 80-inch circumference.

"If a beaver has been fighting, a tiny scar will end up the size of a loonie coin and will cut the price of the pelt in half," he warned. Garry may have joked when he said, "Be a conservationist: eat a beaver a day and save a tree," but he said he was part of the balancing act. Since the fur market fell flat, and therefore trapping, the beaver population exploded to the point that they battled for territory as their numbers increased.

"The role of the trapper is to keep that population in balance with the system," said Garry. "Otherwise, the animals war among themselves and become injured and diseased."

But for Garry and many other people, trapping was a time for getting back to nature. Prices for pelts may well have fallen off over the years, but trapping continued to be part of his life. He recalled evenings in camp when they would play Cut-Throat Euchre, four playing individually, instead of with partners, for a pelt a player, which at that time was $8–10. He told a story about a night long ago when a good-looking well-dressed man entered the camp and joined them during one of the games. When the other players had an opportunity to examine him more closely, they saw that he had cloven hooves...and that the devil was in their midst. Probably a subconscious holdover from Methodist indoctrination.

During the interview, Garry was putting around the bay in his outboard. He pointed to branches high in the trees where children's toys drooped like Spanish Moss hanging on trees in southern Georgia, only here they got that high because that's where they were when the winter snow started to melt. Garry explained that they were the toys of the Bogman's grandchildren. So the legend goes, Bogman was a creature: half frog, half human, who inhabited the waters of Bradley Bay, a creature known to all children whose parents kept them in line by threatening them with being captured by this ogre.

Garry and his wife, Donna, went to camp later that summer in 1990 and Garry found a trap he'd missed picking up in the spring. An otter was in the trap, an animal that Garry has never wanted to trap, so he was sorry and shocked to have been responsible for killing one. That night in camp, when Garry and Donna went to bed, they heard the otters barking— a spooky sound neither of them had ever heard before. And when they left Bradley Bay the next morning, the otters followed them, barking at the boat.

# The Forties

## Alderville School –1942

I realize that the school photograph from 1942 is filled with individuals in the Village, some of whom are still alive and are our elders today.

Top left: Neil Crowe, Carleton Smoke, Doris Lake, Frances Gray, Audrey Marsden, Louella Gray, Nona Simpson, Jean Simpson, Eileen Crowe, Sandford Smoke, Glen Crowe, Max Beaver. John Loukes at back.

Middle left: Catherine Beaver, Maxine Gray, Lillian Bigwin, Elva Crowe, Elgie Marsden, Caroline Marsden, Sheila Crowe, Mary Marsden, Lois Bigwin, Doris Beaver.

Front left: Ken Marsden, Perry Beaver, Roger Crowe, Ted Beaver, Russell Lake, Johnny Lake, Ken Gray, John Crowe

## The Fifties

A page with a few lines from Mary Jane Muskratte Simpson continues from where she had earlier written about women making baskets and other handicrafts *"...but through the fostering hand of the Government other arts are being learned. In 1947, a Homemakers' Club was organized by Mrs. Benson Brant of Tyendenaga, representing the Indian Department. The first [Alderville] President was Mrs. Alfred Simpson, who held that office for four years. She was succeeded by Mrs. James Bigwin Jr.; and the presidency is now occupied by Mrs. John Simpson [1953]. Their aims and objectives are for the better way of life. Sewing is taught, and, at their yearly competitions on the various reserves, demonstrations of many phases of homecraft are given."*

"I was a member of the Homemakers' Club," Gate-gan tells me. "We used to put on all kinds of suppers every year, like we did for the boys when they won the county softball championship. Today they visit the sick in hospital and personally deliver cards of good wishes to community members. Now they bring me birthday cards every year."

**Feast For Champions**—Alderville Trappers Softball Team is feted by the Homemakers' Club at a community feast after winning the East Northumberland Softball League championship in the early 1950s. Bottom row (left to right): Terry Bigwin, Larry Crowe, Jack Loukes (Umpire), Borden Crowe (Manager), Glen Crowe (Field Captain), Pat Mowat. Top row (left to right): John Crowe, Sandy Smoke, Kenneth Marsden, Bob Heafield, Max Beaver, Wally Crowe, Milford (Mel) Smoke, Ted Beaver

The boys seemed to make the best of each season, not just summer, and they took advantage of being in large families with lots of brothers to compete with in sports.

"Their parents didn't have hundreds of dollars to spend on equipment for them like kids get today," Gate-gan says, " but it didn't stop them from playing. Or winning."

**Baseball Team with fans in 1954**

Caroline a.k.a. Granny Fleming (nee Beaver 1871–1956) holding Jan Beaver 1953

Bill Fleming (left) with Vernon Marsden circa 1940s. Caroline Beaver (left) married Joe Fleming, Bill's brother. Caroline's brothers were Bill and George Beaver

**CROWE MAGNUM FORCE 1959**
Roger (left), Wally, Larry & Kingsley Crowe

**THE MARVELLOUS MARSDEN BOYS 1960s**
Ken (left,) Vincent (Peach) & Winston (Babe)

**Preston "Pre" Gray circa 1948**

"Katharine and Preston made a handsome couple," Gate-gan says when we come to their family photographs.

"They had a large family, nine kids. Daughter Caroline says when they stood together, they used to look like stair steps, born virtually one year after the other."

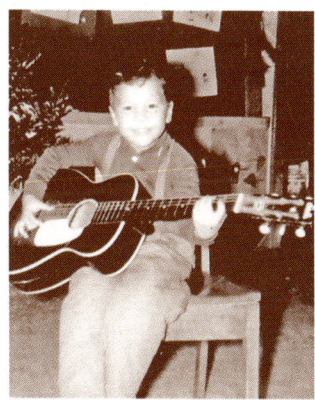

**Doug Gray**, Katharine and Pre's youngest, started playing guitar at a very early age, and today plays guitar as well as banjo and violin. Photo circa 1960s

**Katharine Gray
1950**

**The Crowe and Beaver Kids in 1956**
Wendy Crowe (left), Jan Beaver, Garry Crowe, Pam Crowe, Dave Beaver, Dennis Beaver, Rick Beaver

**Five Gray Kids in 1957** Rod (left), Craig, Hal, Dean and Caroline

## George Beaver 1868-1956

Gate-gan pulls magazines and newspapers from a highly varnished, carved rack next to her rocking chair and hands it to me. "That's George Beaver's work," she tells me. "George Beaver, or Uncle George as the Beaver kids knew him, was a masterful craftsman who supplied each of the children with bows and arrows he made for them when they came to visit. His magazine racks are highly sought after and two were purchased by the Canadian Museum of Civilization. However, their documentation is incorrect in saying that he died in 1910–why, he was the oldest man attending Alderville's 100th anniversary in 1937!

George carved his racks in a sumach grove that he referred to as his parlour. When he had a good stock of them, he tied them on his back and hiked from the Village to sell his work as far away as Stoney Lake.

We are looking at a Weekend Magazine that was published by the Globe & Mail in 1975. The title of the article is How Jack Beaver Got into Power–a clever, ambiguous statement about the kind of man he was and about his work in hydro-electric, then nuclear, power.

## The Man with the Marvelous Tan
## John Wesley Beaver
## 1920-1990

"I was five years old when Jack Beaver was born in 1920," Gate-gan tells me. "Though he accomplished so much in his life it's almost as if he was born an adult. The family was so poor that the kids had to grow up quickly. Jack had three brothers and three sisters, and when they were growing up, their father was living in 'the old way' as they say: he hunted and trapped and guided fishermen. Jack and his brother Delbert used to take a cat to bed with them to keep warm. Some times it was so cold in their house that they'd have to chop through ice in the wash basin to wash in the morning. When they were small kids, Jack and Del used to fish through the ice in Rice Lake during the winter. Often they'd travel up to 10 miles, cutting holes in the ice as they went, catching fish that they'd sell in Roseneath for eight cents a pound. Their dad went off to work in a foundry in Cleveland, ultimately divorced their mother, and Delbert ending up looking after the family."

"Jack Beaver seems to be one student who prospered under Dorcas Atkinson's tutelage at school," I say when I read that he credited her disciplinarian ways with giving him his start in life.

"When he was only 13 years old, Miss Atkinson wanted so much for Jack to try the entrance exam at Cobourg High School that she lent him her treasured fountain pen to write the exam," Gate-gan adds. I read on. He was working in St. Catharines in 1939 when the Royal Air Force was recruiting there, and though he'd only just married Marjorie Marsden a few months previously, he joined and left for England where he flew Spitfire planes in the Battle of Britain and in Europe, and was awarded the King George medal after being injured and sent home in 1944.

"At that time the Department of Veterans' Affairs provided their veterans with either money to build homes, or tuition for them to attend university. Jack opted for more education and got his engineering degree at Queen's University," Gate-gan explains.

Jack joined Ontario Hydro in 1949, was chief at Alderville for four years in the 1950s, and as the article says, "worked his way up through line surveying and maintenance until he was second in command at Rolphton, Canada's first nuclear power station." He later ran the seven million horsepower Churchill Falls plant in Labrador, at that time, "the western world's largest single source of energy" according to journalist Philip Smith. And when the Newfoundland government bought the operation, Jack deferred his retirement and agreed to stay another three years as president of the corporation.

"There's a cute little paragraph about some 'high-pressure think tank' from New York that visited the plant in Churchill Falls, and someone asking where Jack had gotten his marvelous tan. Have you gotten that far?" Gate-gan asks.

"Ya. Here it is. He says, 'from my ancestors'."

**Beaver Family in 1949**
Wayne (left), Dennis, Rick held by Jack beside wife Marjorie Beaver. A complete family portrait would include daughter Janet and son Dave who came along later

# The Sixties

**Young Bucks**—From left: Barry Marsden, aka "Buckshot", Paul Simpson, aka "Gran", Garry Crowe, aka "Ga" and Dennis Simpson, aka "Doing"

Gate-gan has bundled the next three decades in separate file folders. They are significantly slimmer than other earlier decades. I wonder about this and as if Gate-gan is reading my mind, she answers for me.

"Television. That's what became popular during these decades, starting in the 1950s, though a very few people had them here in the Village. But when they became affordable, everyone had a big one-eyed wooden box plunked front and centre in their livingroom, like a long lost member of the family, one they looked at even if it wasn't turned on. I suspect that's why there aren't as many photographs. The television took them all. It became a babysitter for kids when they came home from school, and became the centre of attention every evening. Terrible invention. No one tells stories anymore. They let the television do it for them." Gate-gan's arms are crossed and she has a stern look on her face. I am holding the file from the 1960s and pull out a school photograph.

"Here's Jack Loukes again," I say, handing Gate-gan the photo, making her uncross her arms and lighten up a little bit. "He has certainly been present, almost from the beginning."

"He taught for 28 years and he was a good athlete," says Gate-gan. "Those two interests alone would count for a lot of photographs in this trunk. They say he was a traditional teacher until it came time for recess, and I guess he got the boys into boxing–instead of fighting."

**"Those Who Stayed For Lunch"** ...
one summer's day in the 1960s

Mrs. Master and John Loukes in back row
Boys left to right: Dean Gray, Dennis Simpson, Hal Gray, Ron Gray, Rod Gray, Paul Simpson, Craig Gray
Girls left to right: Dorothy Bigwin, Pam Crowe, Wendy Crowe, Jan Smoke, Nancy Marsden, Gaye Marsden, Trudy Marsden

Outfielder-Pitcher Craig Gray "Belted grand-slam homer in Orphans' wacky win at Napanee May 28, 1971

Circa 1990

**Kingsley Crowe** (left) or "King, one of Borden's sons, moved to Akron, Ohio, in 1945 at age 18 after a hockey and softball career in Canada. He was inducted into the Greater Akron Baseball Hall of Fame for his contribution to baseball in the area where he played from 1946-1963, playing on the Krispy Kreme team from 1954-1960

## Alton & Fran Bigwin

A couple of articles about Alton Bigwin are in the Sixties file, along with a photograph of him and his wife, Fran, taken at a going-away party held in the Village before they left for Germany in 1968.

"Alton and Fran live in the Village now," Gate-gan tells me, "but he and his family lived off the reserve for many years. Look at this article's headline: 'Alton Bigwin Conquers the City... and more.' You betcha. He was even written about in a book. His mother Mae must have been proud of him. He was quite an athlete too." I read on.

Alton attended Cobourg Collegiate from 1943-1947. Alton enfranchised in order to use the enfranchisement money to attend university. He was accepted at Queen's University in Kingston where he received his Bachelor of Arts, and later his Master of Education at the University of Toronto. His first school was in Arden, Ontario, Fran's home town. Later, he taught for six years in schools in Crowland, Lakefield and Perth before becoming a principal.

He was principal at North Bendale Public School in the 1960s, and in 1964, the year the Beatles came to Toronto for the first time, he took his wife and four daughters north to work on a reserve for summer school.

Fran recalls having promised the girls that they could go back for the Beatles' concert. But once they'd settled in their summer home, the girls didn't think they wanted to go back to the city. "Their decision was quite a positive statement for them to make about their new landscape–and they didn't want to leave their Dad there alone." And Alton learned the realities of trapping versus education. He returned to Toronto that fall, and in 1966 became principal of Wm. G. Miller School in Scarborough.

In 1967, the United Church of Canada published a book by Isobel McFadden entitled, THEY WALK IN DIGNITY: Four Indian Canadians: Adam Fiddler, Nellie Jacobson, Nathan Montour and Alton Bigwin. On page 42 Alton tells the author, "My life at Alderville was much like anyone's life in a rural town. We were just as able as any boys and girls to fit into advanced education and city jobs. Sure we had to go in to the collegiate by bus, but so do all kids in the country. My own children, of course, know no other kind of life than city life, education and city jobs."

A newspaper reporter writes, "As a father of four daughters and one son, Mr. Bigwin is intensely interested in teaching. As an Ojibway involved in the Indian-Eskimo Association and the Toronto Indian Centre, he can see some progress in meeting the particular needs of children in the bigger centres. We want to see this sort of thing happening in even the remotest communities and certainly this is a step in the right direction."

From 1968-1970, Alton was "on loan" to the D.N.D. schools in Baden, West Germany. In 1970, in Lahr, a son joins the Bigwin family. Shortly after returning to Canada, Alton was invited to work in the Curriculum Branch of the Ministry of Education where he served for 10 years before retiring. Subsequently, for another six years, Alton served on the Ontario Board of Parole.

" And he's still active," I tell Gate-gan. "He's in our Ojibway language class."

# The Seventies

The next set of documents Gate-gan has put together appeared to help illustrate that heritage was experiencing a rebirth in 1973 in Alderville. As part of the Native Enrichment Programme at Roseneath Centennial School, a curriculum guide was published. The same year, Dr. Walter Kenyon of the Royal Ontario Museum began an archeological dig on East Sugar Island, enlisting help from students at the school, which became "a turning point for their pride in being Indian." The students learned from taking soil samples on the island that their ancestors had been growing wild rice *(zizania palustris)* for more than 9000 years. Dr. Kenyon and botanist Dr. J. McAndrews claimed that its growth had reached a peak and began to wane about the beginning of the Christian era. Isn't that ironic?

In addition to a cultural renaissance, the hockey and baseball teams were doing really well too. Merrill Crowe was racing cars and winning lots of trophies. By the end of his competitive career racing, playing hockey, and pitching horseshoes, Merrill's Wall of Fame in his garage covered most bare space with his awards. He had so many he often removed his name plaque and recycled trophies as prizes for local competitions.

Merrill Crowe in 1973 with his car racing trophies

**"Alderville Senior Hockey Team wins Southern Ontario All-Indian Championship"** Receiving trophy for their team in 1971 are (left) Winston (Babe) Marsden, Glen Crowe (manager) and Merrill Crowe. Team members: Winston Marsden, Rick Beaver, Bob Heafield, Craig Gray, Bruce Nichols, Clayton Smoke, Glen Crowe, Merrill Crowe, Garry Crowe, and Wendel McCue

**Alderville Indians 1975 Baseball Champs**
Top row left: Ken Marsden, Ralph Smoke, Ron Gray, Craig Gray, Babe Marsden. Front row left: Jamie Marsden, Rob Brown, Kenny Marsden, Terry Smoke, Jeff Beaver

## The Eighties

**The Wandering Ended**

Artists Hal Gray & Rick Beaver

John Crowe

    The mementos from the 1980s in Gate-gan's trunk were photographs illustrating the fine art that was emerging in the Village. It seems that in 1983 Chief John Crowe commissioned Alderville artists Rick Beaver and Hal Gray to paint a mural. Entitled "The Wandering Ended," the acrylic panel celebrates the return and settlement of the Mississauga Ojibways to an area they had inhabited 300 years earlier.
    Today it hangs in the Alderville community centre.

# When The Real Wandering Ended—1985

Gate-gan rubs one of the many faint, white scars on her arm. She is looking beyond the walls of this house, to some scene that makes her eyes misty, her expression serene. It is as if rubbing her arm is like rubbing the legendary genie's lamp, memories seem to surface in her mind's eye.

"What do you see, Gate-gan?" I ask.

"I'm seeing flashes, images from my stay in the hospital after the car accident we were in, what, 22 years ago, just before you were born. It was 1983. I remember that for sure because it was just before Bill C-31 became law, and that issue had been on my mind a lot.

"I lay in a ward with nine other women, many of them from different Native cultures, some from different parts of the world. I remember lying there, looking at the women, and myself. Our pains were different, that was for sure, but beneath the clean hospital sheets, the same open-backed cotton gowns, we were all pretty much the same. We would all receive medicines from the same nurse. Some were young, some old and wrinkled, but we would all be served by the same orderly. The more I thought about it while I was lying there, I realized that all has not been equal in the Native woman's world. Lying in bed had given me time to think about it more rationally. The women's ward and the nursery both gave me perspective on a much larger picture.

"From a bed near the window, the clouded eyes of an aged Indian woman gazed out at a vision I knew only she could see beyond the obscured, treeless horizon of smoke-stacks and sky-scrapers. The old woman's gnarled nut-brown hands would often draw the covers around her withered body and free the braid of her snow white hair from the bedclothes. Once these misshapen fingers had been nimble; her white hair had shone like a raven's feathers in the sunlight. Her Indian name was actually Raven. However crippled she was, her fingers would plait the locks of her hair in a memory of their own, while her lips moved in silent prayer.

"Each night when the lights were turned off, I often heard murmurs coming from different corners of the room. In the darkness it seemed there was a privacy, a protected secrecy; there was a safeness in the strange darkness where together in the long rows of beds each woman separately owned her own pain and suffering. At dawn's light we exchanged recipes for conjuring joy, making antidotes for sorrow, for raising each other's spirits.

"One night in that safe darkness, the nurses made their rounds, some carrying flashlights, to check on their sleeping charges. They found that the ancient one, Raven, had passed on. The other women had been aware that something was happening in the room but had been lulled back to their dreams where hospital sounds were reinterpreted to compliment the dream like a soundtrack. In the morning, the old woman's absence was obvious to everyone when they awoke. There was an empty bed, ready for another patient.

"In 1983, when Raven died, she had to be buried in a non-Native graveyard. Even though she had been born on a reservation, her husband had enfranchised decades before and they had moved off the reserve. Even though the old woman's husband had died many years before her, she still wasn't welcome, couldn't live or die on the reserve. Until 1985, none of her children or grandchildren had Indian status." Gate-gan continues to massage her arm, thinking back. "Raven and I had many conversations about the old days and family life. We joked about Indian women inventing the first disposable diapers and sanitary napkins from moss. When bark from a tree was used before plastic had been invented.

"The day after Raven died, I had an urge to see babies: the beginning of life. The nursery was on the floor below the women's ward, and one of the nurses walked down with me. The babies were all asleep in plastic boxes. Bundled, they all looked the same through the glass. The hair was longer and thicker on some, lighter or darker on others, but they all received the same attention and care each day. They all cried with the same exuberance. While I was there, one fair-skinned babe awoke first. His blue eyes tried to focus on a band of colour printed on the plastic box. I recognized the name on the baby's box. Indian. The little guy didn't know it, but his future would be distinctly different than the other fair-haired babies delivered here. His mother had married an Indian, and this child would have the Indian status of his father. The name on the box beside him was Anderson, and I could see a dark little head peaking out from beneath a pink delivery blanket. Her mother was probably Native, and she would not have any status on her mother's former reserve...not for another two years. Just like you, Katie."

I suddenly remember Gate-gan telling me years ago that one of the first to return to Alderille was Nora Bothwell. She had been married to a non-Native and later became divorced. A single mother of two, she moved back and was elected chief shortly after, the first woman chief in the band's 150-year history. Immediately she started caring for her new extended family of 582. The impact of Bill C-31 was three times greater than anyone had expected. In 1987, headlines in a local weekly newspaper read, "Housing Crisis Leaves Indian Families Homeless." Well, that was an editor's sensationalist approach. They already had homes off the reserve—whether they owned or rented them, but with Bill C-31's revision, it meant that people *wanted* to move back to their ancestral home. In 1988, the same paper reported that 70 families were on a waiting list for housing in Alderville.

Chief Nora Bothwell and Councilor Penny Crowe in 1988

## Rick Beaver

Circa 1984

"That's Jack and Marjorie Beaver's son," Gate-gan points to a photograph of Rick Beaver. Well, Gate-gan didn't have to tell me that. I mean I know Rick. He lives in the Village. And I know his history. Rick studied science at university, getting his bachelor's at the University of Guelph and his master's at the University of Alberta, in biology. Both he and his sister Janet were trained biologists and their brother Dave works for the Ministry of Natural Resources in wildlife and fisheries management. Rick later worked as a wildlife biologist in all of the western provinces with the Canadian Wildlife Service and had his own consulting business.

His scientific career took a sharp turn in the 1970s when he attended a Native artist's exhibition in a gallery in Edmonton. It inspired him so much that he embarked on his new artistic journey and by the 1980s had moved back to Alderville and was painting full-time. He started a publishing company called Sweetgrass Studios, to publish his limited edition prints.

In 1984, Rick met Dawn MacDonald, and with her and others, and with the support of several Native artists, they founded Village AID: Village-to Village Applied Integrated Development, in response to the famine crisis that Ethiopia was suffering. What came out of it was a twinning project wherein indigenous artists were twinned with countries in Africa for which they painted poster-sized paintings. Villagers, a magazine, was published, featuring their art and reports on the progress of the project. Several artists attended the Commonwealth Conference in Vancouver, thanks to fundraising by the people of Alderville. Six months later, Rick was in Nairobi, meeting with 50 African environment ministers. Ultimately, the exhibit of 41 paintings by 26 indigenous artists was purchased from Villagers in 1991 by the Grand Council of the Crees (of Quebec).

In 1987, Rick moved to British Columbia and continued producing limited edition prints. He was invited on a celebrity artist whale watch from which Rick has painted many images and was featured in many exhibitions. In 1996, he came home to build the physical structure, Sweetgrass Studios, his studio and gallery here in the Village. His passion got the best of him in 2000, when he was instrumental in having the Black Oak Savanna Tallgrass Prairie here designated as a heritage site, and subsequently was appointed coordinator of the site, a position he held until his health forced him to resign in 2004, and return his focus to his art.

"And, boy, has he focussed," Gate-gan says when I look up from his clippings and photographs. "You can find his designs all over the world, on scarves and umbrellas and all kinds of things."

"And he isn't limiting himself to painting on paper or canvas," I add. "I attended Port Hope's Earth Day event in 2005 where Rick built a sculpture, he calls them ephemeral sculptures because he uses natural, found materials. So far, I hear that he's made them in Algonquin Park, on the west coast of Vancouver Island, in Costa Rica and in Mexico."

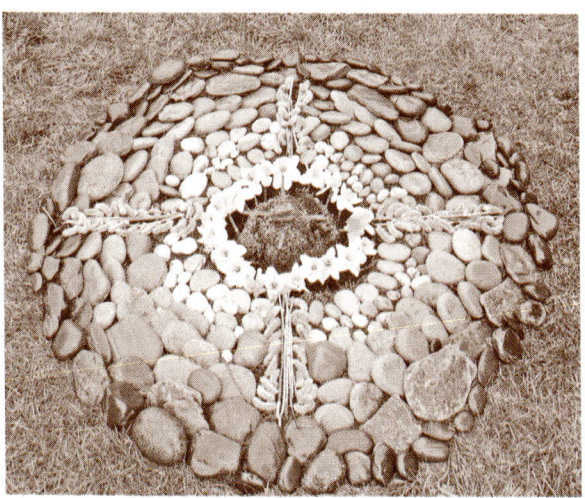

**2005 Earth Day Sculpture** in Port Hope
Materials used were beach stones, Pussy Willow catkins, hawthorns, daffodils, Cardinal feathers and stems of Queen Anne's Lace

# Hal Gray

I recognize the shots of Hal and Maureen Gray, taken in 1989. One of his paintings hangs in our living-room. Hal has carved, he's made puppets, and of course, he paints in acrylic and pen and ink. Gate-gan leans forward and looks at the photographs.

"I remember Hal telling a journalist the reason behind his idea to teach children about their Ojibway heritage. He explained that a kid had come up to him and asked what kind of Indian he was. Hal had replied that he was a good Indian.

"But that didn't satisfy the youngster," Gate-gan plumped the pillow on the chesterfield. "And that was inspiration and reason for him to teach the course. He and Maureen have nurtured young people as foster parents and as supportive members of the community all their adult lives."

## The Nineties

**May The Force Be With You**—RCMP Officer Eric Crowe (left), his first cousins OPP officers Suzanne and Jennifer and their father, Wally Crowe

**Wally Crowe** in 1990. Wally worked as an Ontario Provincial Police officer for 28 years, six years on Manitoulin Island and 22 years at the Lindsay detachment. He retired in 1993. His daughter, Suzanne is now a Sergeant and teaches at the Police Academy in Orillia, Ontario

**Rick Beaver** puts the finishing touches on "An Evening Thought", a print commissioned in 1995 by Ontario Hydro for recipients of the **John Welsey Beaver Awards**, in honour of Rick's father who was a manager at Ontario Hydro for 20 years. The annual scholarship promotes Native students' entry into post secondary education

**Men's War Canoe Race 1990** Centre front from left: Larry Crowe Jr., Dave Mowat, Clint Crowe, Howie Crowe
Canoe to right of centre: From left: Jim Bob Marsden, Patrick Mattson, Joe Cormier, John Mattson

Chef Penny Crowe cooks hamburgers while son Kyle supervises

Jim Bob Marsden at 1990 Jamboree

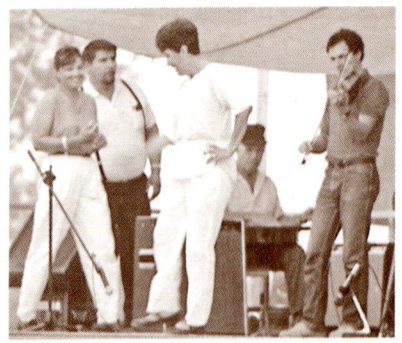

Holly Crowe (left) waits her turn to stepdance while Caroline Powers steps, with emcee Dave Simpson in background. Dave Mowat (right) plays harmonica with Mel Blaker looking on

Randy checks his printer's output for "Respect," a print he is producing from the original painting in the background

## Randy Paul Smoke

"That's Bean, eh?" I ask Gate-gan to confirm the photograph of a man painting a scene on a large canvas.

"Yes, that's Randy Paul Smoke. Oh, he was a tall drink of water when he was growing up. Like a string bean, hence the name Bean that has stuck with him ever since. He's filled out a bit more now. I was happy to hear after all those years working in construction that he decided to pursue his lifelong dream of being an artist. It wasn't fashionable when he was growing up. It wasn't cool to be artistic; it was akin to being a sissy. Nor was it lucrative. Guess he'd heard too many starving artist stories. So he worked in construction and earned good money but after a few too many injuries, he decided to chase his dream."

In 1989, Randy started to paint under the tutelage of Norm Green, a realist painter up the road in Hastings. Randy says that he tried to duplicate Green's work, but would always add something, the truth, he called it. He says he paints with both sides of his brain. Randy spent two years with Green and then Green told him to go off and study his Native culture and paint that.

According to Gate-gan, Bean loves to tell stories but no one has the time or interest to listen. This way, he can paint the stories, talk about old people and about ceremonies through his paintings.

In 2000, he attended the White Mountain Academy of Fine Arts in Elliot Lake and spent two years learning nothing more than art history, but at least he was in an artistic environment. In 2003, he was one of two from Canada to be accepted in the Fine Arts programme at the Institute of American Indian Art in Santa Fe, New Mexico, where he was exposed to the best artists in the world. In addition to painting, he learned to make jewelry from Navajo master craftspeople.

Now he uses his paintings as tools when he visits schools and tells stories about the scenes he has recreated. Kind of like a realistic visual history lesson.

A Good Place to Gather mural by Randy Paul Smoke in 2001 hangs in the Alderville Community Centre

## The New Millennium: 2000

"I am grateful to the Creator that I lived long enough to see the new millennium and the positive energy that seems to be stirring around here," Gate-gan says as she rocks and sips her tea. I'm sorting through photographs of very recent events, some of which I have been involved in or at least know about.

Little did anyone know at the time, that in settling us here on land that no settler could farm, because of our traditional practices we have kept one of the largest pieces of rare savanna/tallgrass prairies in southern Ontario, and with it many rare and endangered plants, insects, animals and birds. On the eve of the new millennium, a portion of land here was designated a Natural Heritage site. The savanna has been managed since then, it continues to be studied and has become a destination for many nature enthusiasts, botanists and other academics. Two editions of a book about the site have been published, both entitled TO KNOW THIS PLACE: The Black Oak Savanna/Tallgrass Prairie of Alderville First Nation. Gate-gan has them both and lent the first edition to me when I did a project on it in college last year and our class came down to take a tour.

"Look at those figures, would you," Gate-gan leans forward when I come to the report she has saved from the Ontario Ministry of Education, a survey that was conducted in 2001, ranking townships and municipalities in Northumberland County. It appears that Alderville, compared to the other municipalities, had the lowest number of single parents. And while it also had the lowest average income, Alderville scored the highest, 72.3%, of its children had attained post secondary education, or higher.

"And in addition to having the most children with higher education than the rest, I heard somewhere that Alnwick township has the highest number of artists per capita in Ontario. And Alderville has a good number of them," I tell her, even though I think she probably already knows.

The Alderville group stands atop Sugar Island after paddling one of the 10 war canoes from Curve Lake, Stoney Lake, down the Trent River, through Lakefield and Peterborough, en route to their final destination at Vimy Ridge, on the shores of Rice Lake and Alderville First Nation.

Back row: Caley Detweiler (left), Philip Beaver, Kevin Wingard, Lori Crowe. Middle row: Patrick Smoke (left), Rick Beaver, Eric Crowe with Darlene Solomon in front, Clint Crowe with Amber Crowe in front, Jeff Beaver with Sheri Beaver in front. Bottom row: Chance Anderson (left), Joe Martin, Jason Marsden, John Mattson

## Pulling Together 2004

RCMP Officer Eric Crowe was instrumental in bringing PULLING TOGETHER to Alderville in 2004, an initiative that started in British Columbia several years ago with the police and First Nations who included the youth of their communities in this celebratory, yet grueling, trip that follows the routes of their ancestors.

Elder Rick Beaver (right) met the canoes when they reached Sugar Island, and granted them all permission to land. They climbed up the muddy hillside to gather in a circle for a ceremony during which Rick was presented with a blanket. In gratitude, he sang in Ojibway and drummed for them

**Asking Permission to Leave Sugar Island**

Traditionally, when war canoes approached a village, they asked permission to come ashore...and often backed their sterns in first, to indicate that they were not aggressive. Similarly, when departing, it was proper etiquette to ask permission to leave

**Approaching Vimy**–Eric Crowe at stern, Darlene Solomon, Jasmine Kabestra-Savage, Madison Ready, Kyle Tuttle, Dave Fougere, Jeremy Whetung, Anthony Cameron at bow

# John Loukes
# 1911-2002

    I've come to an interview a journalist had with John Loukes in 1989, entitled There's No Turning Back, in which Mr. Loukes says, "Tradition is gone from here, and its return is just about as likely as farmers going back to the pioneer days." Sixteen years have passed since he made that statement, much has occurred since then, and though he is no longer with us, I wonder what he would have to say today.
    "What do you think of that statement, Gate-gan?" I ask.
    "Well, he was right when he said that it's part of life for a minority group, which we are, dominated by those whose culture survives. I've had long talks with John over the years about this subject, and what was interesting to both of us is the way a dominant society judges a people: you're civilized if you conform to their ways. We may not be able to turn back the hands of time, but at least now we can celebrate our traditions. And as you no doubt notice, many non-Native people from the dominant society are attending our socials, powwows and cultural events, so they must see value in our old ways." I continue to read about the man who figures so prominently throughout Alderville's recent history.

Apparently, John Loukes' grandfather spoke Ojibway and his father, William, was just learning the Native language at school when the British system put an end to any utterance of it in the classroom or schoolyard. Deadening. Glad I wasn't around then.

The journalist writes that Mr. Loukes has often been described as being witty and it is assumed that he is an extrovert—at least in his own home, but he claims it was not always thus. One of the ironies of John Loukes' life is that he taught at the Alderville School for 28 years, but had had no fondness for school as a child, he said. His father was a farmer by day and a barber by night. His grandfather, "half English", operated the post office across from the monument. All of the other kids' parents were hunters and trappers, and he had no knowledge of this way of life. "My mother practised the arts of peace, living a life other than nomadic. And my father didn't come under the influence of the rest," Mr. Loukes explained in the interview. His mother died when he was three, after giving birth to a fourth child who later died of whooping cough.

His grandmother was 60 when his mother died. John, his two remaining siblings and his father went to live with his grandparents. His feelings of shyness developed out of the exclusion from the rest at the Alderville School. This shyness continued when he attended high school in Cobourg and later in Campbellford, getting his education as he needed it, he said.

"I was just a little curio," he recalled. "I knew a lot of the answers but was scared of being wrong." He overcame his shyness when he was elected president of the literary society at the Campbellford High School.

"I got more confidence. I had hated oral composition," he recalled. "My lips would freeze." The literary society presented commencement performances in which he actually sang and danced. "Performing gave me confidence, and the inspiration I got from acting allowed me to ad lib in the scripts." His wife, Elizabeth Loukes, remembered her mother seeing him perform.

"She told me she liked the constable in the play. It was John Loukes," says Elizabeth.

He later attended teachers' college or Normal, as it was then called, in Peterborough. "Something happened there. We were all strangers and I completely overcame my basic shyness." And never looked back, it would seem.

Mr. Loukes' first inkling of discrimination slapped him in the face when he applied for his premier teaching position in Yelverton, Ontario. "They had a stereotyped image of Native people and didn't hire me," he said. "It was then I made up my mind I would stick with Native people." His sensitivity obviously remained much a part of him, highlighted in the anecdotes he used to illustrate his approach to teaching and consulting with his people throughout his career.

"I didn't see the cultural differences in the young people that other (older) people feared. We started a young people's society while I was at the school in Alderville and lived in the manse. We put on shows and invited the parents. It kept me young; I still feel like a young person. We got along well." It was working with young people that kept him teaching. Students liked Jack Loukes as a teacher; he let them follow their interests in sports, and gave them time in the boxing ring. But he left in 1964 when he was asked to be principal. "I'm not a person who thrives on stress," he said. He left to join the Department of Indian Affairs first as a councilor in the London office, working in education and post education placement there, and later in Ottawa. And there his knowledge, sensitivity and understanding served him well.

Other teachers couldn't understand why a good student who was doing so well would disappear from college before it ended in April or May, to return to the North. Mr. Loukes understood. He'd flown over their tundra and seen the flocks of Canada Geese that arrived each year at that time. "Hunting is a very big part of their life," he explained.

He made sure that students really wanted to do what they said, and that it was not what their parents had planned for them. "We had two kinds of tests: one for aptitude and one for interest, because sometimes aptitude tests were culturally slanted." While co-workers said they shouldn't overeducate them, Mr. Loukes sought each individual's potential. He'd seen the exploitation of young Native people arriving in Ottawa-Hull from the North. "They couldn't speak English and they couldn't speak French, and when they tried to speak, people thought they were drunk and would have them arrested. I set the police straight, and there were no more arrests."

After three attempts, Mr. Loukes retired successfully from the Department of Indian Affairs in 1977. During his failed attempts, he worked for Alderville, Hiawatha and Curve Lake bands as education liaison officer, and assisted in off-reserve housing.

As he cast an objective eye over the world, one thing that stood out in his mind is the return to the spiritual realm, he told the journalist.

"You can see the effects of corporate greed; society is now becoming more closely attuned to nature. In the old days, men would live by making crafts and many of the men were known for the axe handles they carved, to exchange for food and supplies. They took pride in their work. It was their artistic expression." On the Alderville First Nation Reserve, hunting and fishing have become leisure activities, according to Mr. Loukes. "There's no shortage of food, and men take holidays, time off work, to go hunting. But there is no way to return to the past," he said.

While there is an interest in learning the Native language in school today, Mr. Loukes said it is impossible for the students to become fluent unless there is total immersion. Nor will tradition be preserved as long as Alderville's numbers are small and it is close to other cultures. (We couldn't be closer with a highway running through the Village.)

"That's why Curve Lake retained their language and tradition," he said. "The roads were bad, and a significant number of them lived there. When we went there as kids, they used to call us white Indians. Culture gets diluted in each generation," he said. "People try to hang on to old ways, but they can't make a living at it so they have to adapt. All of us."

"He's right, you have to admit," says Gate-gan.

"Oh, I can't argue with him on most things," I agree, "but I think our culture has strengthened over the years, not become diluted. That you can study your own language and heritage from public school through university, actually get a doctorate for doing it and not be enfranchised, well, that's a strong culture, don't you think?"

"I do." She leaned over and kissed my cheek. "And that is why I am giving you this trunk."

## Epilogue

After Gate-gan and I had finally emptied the trunk of its contents, small mountains of binders, photographs and sheaves of paper had sprung up all over the living and dining rooms. I would take my time to file them all appropriately. But for the moment, my attention is focused inside the empty trunk. I must look like I am a discerning crafts-person, inspecting its construction.

"Who ever made this put thin layers of cedar strapping on both the inside of the lid and the floor of the trunk," I comment to Gate-gan. At the edge of one of these straps, a fleck of colour catches my eye.

"Did you notice this paper stuffed in under the slats, Gate-gan?"

"Never. After all these years," Gate-gan says, relaxing in her favourite rocking chair, smoothing the folds in her cotton housedress.

"It looks like an old school notebook." I try to pry it free, poking at it, but it won't budge. Armed with a knife from the cutlery drawer, and with some effort, I am able to extract a greasy primer notebook from under the slats.

*"My diary. A gift from my best friend, Hester Ann Hubbard Case, Christmas 1829"* is scrawled in deliberate round writing, now barely legible on the book's cover.

"This is Sarah's diary," I whisper, barely able to breathe. Holding the notebook in both hands, I sit down on the chesterfield near Gate-gan.

"Hettie has written something to Sarah in Ojibway," I continue to whisper, though I don't know why. "Such tiny handwriting."

Gate-gan fills our mugs with her famous high-octane tea, and rocks, smiling at me, waiting for my translation.

"Well, here goes. Gee, she doesn't call her Sarah.

*"To my dear Ishpiniibin. I hope you will use this book as a diary, a record for your thoughts, for your impressions of the world, and for your knowledge of the truth as we all should know it. With all my love and respect, Hettie.'*

"I have read about this woman." I stare at the woman's spidery script. "I read somewhere that she died of depression. A long, lingering death was how it was described. I wonder what that was all about?"

Gate-gan takes another sip of her tea before she speaks.

"I will rest assured you'll make it your business to find out, Katie."